NOT A GAMES PERSON

Julie Myerson

YELLOW JERSEY PRESS
LONDON

Published by Yellow Jersey Press 2005

2 4 6 8 10 9 7 5 3 1

Copyright © Julie Myerson 2005

Julie Myerson has asserted her right under the Copyright, Designs
and Patents Act 1988 to be identified as the author of this work

First published in Great Britain in 2005 by
Yellow Jersey Press

Yellow Jersey Press
Random House, 20 Vauxhall Bridge Road,
London SW1V 2SA

Random House Australia (Pty) Limited
20 Alfred Street, Milsons Point, Sydney,
New South Wales 2061, Australia

Random House New Zealand Limited
18 Poland Road, Glenfield,
Auckland 10, New Zealand

Random House South Africa (Pty) Limited
Endulini, 5A Jubilee Road, Parktown 2193,
South Africa

The Random House Group Limited Reg. No. 954009
www.randomhouse.co.uk

A CIP catalogue record for this book
is available from the British Library

ISBN 0–224–07399–0

Papers used by Random House are natural, recyclable products made from wood grown in
sustainable forests. The manufacturing processes conform to the environmental regulations of
the country of origin

Printed and bound in Great Britain by
Clays Ltd, St Ives plc

For Raph — because he is a games person!

This is me. Six years old and standing in a sack in the middle of a field somewhere in the middle of England a long time ago.

I don't know why I'm here or what I'm doing — I don't have any idea what the purpose is of standing in this field, all I know is they want me to jump — hold the sack up as tight as I can and jump jump jump to the finishing line.

I'm surrounded by people but all alone. There's a horrible feeling in my tummy and an itch on my leg, like a fly crawling over it. I shiver and wait for a whistle to blow.

Just looking at the finish line gives me a tight feeling all over. Don't think about it. All right I won't. I'll look somewhere else instead. Up there is a good place. Crick my neck and up there suddenly, up in the dirty hot sky, there's a bird — could be any sort of swifty sharp-feathered bird — but you can tell it's going somewhere far far away, could be anywhere — Africa and Egypt and Asia Minor, the places in the spelling test. It's someone else's sky, the bird's sky and I wish it was mine too and that I was going with it, far away from here — from this sack this field and this stupid and perplexing day which, if the bird looks down, it won't even have the faintest idea is called Sports Day.

*

This is the story of a girl who lost a race. Who loses all races. A girl who cannot run or jump or fight or speak up in class or even, in fact, put herself forward or stand up to be counted in any way.

A girl with kinked mouse hair and stick legs and skinny raw knees and a head full of lunatic ideas she dare not voice. A girl who has big feet and a lively face and an eager, wiry body but no killer instinct whatsoever. A girl who is afraid, always afraid, not of losing but of daring to make the big and terrifying statement that is competing.

*

Because the world has rules – complicated, harsh, mystifying rules – I am a nervous child. Mostly afraid. Light, delicate, nervy and afraid – so afraid – of breaking the rules when I'm not looking, by mistake.

So I stay alert, I can't ever relax. If I don't stay tense and pay attention there will be something I never knew or didn't realise that will seem to come out of nowhere and then my heart will swerve and I will go red or wet myself or die. My heart will beat so fast it will spiral off the edge of my body and stop. Dead. And so I live with the fear that any minute now someone will ask me to do something I don't know how to do, ask me to remember something I never even knew in the first place. A lesson I was absent from, a method I missed, an idea I never fully understood. And then I will be stuck, blank, I won't know how. Then what will happen?

Fire, suffocation, drowning, bleeding, laughter, scorn, death. These are the consequences of relaxing.

Home – I like home. I know the rules of family, of home. They are calm and unchanging and they make a warm and even kind of sense to me, even though sometimes I get punished. Slap on the hand, or the high jump which means a smack bottom or straight to bed. Sometimes a spanking with the smooth side of a hairbrush.

'That didn't hurt,' I say. But it did hurt, it does, and when I'm not feeling furious then I try to believe what they say: that they only do it because they love me.

At home there are curtains and towels and bedspreads and piles of soft clean things that feel and smell right. At home someone is always there to pick you up and say, There, there. My baby sister fell into the flower beds and got scratched by roses – bright, surprising criss-crosses of blood even through her nappy – but apart from that, as long as you don't touch the stove and as long as you hold on when you go downstairs, there are no dangers at home. At home you flourish and grow, even when you're naughty. Because at home you didn't mean it and you'll do better next time and you're trying and you're punished for your own sake. I'd like to stay at home for all my life, live there and be there and sleep in my own bed and be my Mum's helper and never have to go out into the Big Girl's World. That would be my ideal life. The life of the Ladybird Key Words Reading Scheme.

'My Little Helper,' says Mummy as she pegs out the tea towels on the wavy, blowing line, 'my Princess and my Helper and my Little Friend, Jules, that's what you are.'

My best thing is delivering the milk. Father Christmas brought my lorry and it has four wheels and a yellow string to pull it. Every day I go along the floor to where my Mum is washing up and I look up at her with her hands wiggling around right there in the middle of the bubbles and I say: 'How many pints today?'

And she says in a special casual voice as if she doesn't know me, 'Three please.'

'Three?'

'Yes thanks a lot.'

And I put the three white plastic bottles on the step near her feet and then I walk back to the sofa. Very slow and a bit fed up like a real grown-up doing work. But inside my heart swoops and sings with the fun of it: I've just delivered the milk!

*

If you don't join in, you get nowhere in life. That's what her Mum says. And she should know. She flew to boarding school on the Isle of Man when she was five, had her mouth washed out with soap for swearing at seven, left school at fifteen, married at twenty. And yet her Mum has always played the game, has always joined in, has always been tough in the face of competition. Her Mum is beautiful, proud, fierce, strong. When she went to boarding school she lied and told them she was a princess. Princess Maritza. They almost believed her.

But this girl, her daughter, is not tough, is not beautiful or brave or strong. And she doesn't even care about it, well not very much. She could never even begin to pass herself off as a princess. She is a girl who doesn't want to come Second, Third or even First. Especially not First. More than anything, she wishes she could disappear, that she didn't have to be there in the first place. This is a girl who, when faced with a ball hurtling her way, will always do the same thing: turn and run as fast as she possibly can in the opposite direction.

*

Here is a photo of a baby, a sweet and tender weeks-old baby in a white dress snugged unmoving across its Mummy's shoulder, so small and young that its face is bunched into a duckling pout, fat lips, breast-milk breath, fingers curled, legs struggling in white woollen bootees, not yet ready to crawl or walk or run.

The baby is safe. No one is asking it to enter any races yet. The baby is stuck into the album with silver corners, frozen safely and for ever on her Mummy's shoulder in July 1960.

'You were a lovely baby,' my Mum says with a little sigh. 'When you came along, it was like I suddenly had a friend, first time in my life I wasn't lonely. I called you my Princess, my Sweetheart, my little Teddy Bear.'

*

Here I am – my first thoughtless movements. I kick. I gasp. I stretch out my hands. You would not know, looking at me in my carrycot, that I am not going to be competitive in the slightest. There are no clues that this baby with her white knitted bootees and slightly sallow skin will be the last one to be picked for netball, the one that no one wants on their team.

When the baby moves, everyone says aaah. When she falls asleep in her carrycot with her hands bunched in the air, like flowers, they say, Look! Look at her little hands! – as if they've never seen hands before. When she wakes, she kicks her feet in ferocious, gasping silence for a while before the kicks grow more urgent and her breath seems to come undone and she wails. Someone always picks her up at this point, rescues her from herself.

When the baby gets up on her knees and rocks, they all say, Oh look, look at her, what she's doing! When the baby shuffles along on her bottom or her belly, everyone looks pleased and interested. She smiles. A long thin line of dribble hangs from her lower lip and keeps on going till it touches the floor.

The baby sits in her high chair and throws a blue poodle on the floor. When it hits the ground she peers over and laughs and laughs. A grown-up hand places it briskly back on her tray. She throws it again, laughs again. Her first sport. Poodle-throwing.

*

But — just look at her, this child in the sack in the field. Short brown hair cut straight round the ears like a boy's (not her choice by the way). Quite blue eyes which, if you look closer, have a felt-tipped band of dark around the iris, purplish lips slightly chapped and sore, big bunny front teeth flecked with white (from when she had the measles, very badly, one Christmas), bitten nails and the boniest knees you've ever seen. Bony and scabbed and bruised. She thinks they look like boy's knees. They do look like boy's knees.

But it's worse than that. Big feet — big for her age and her size. She hates them. Good for tennis is what the grown-ups all say with their loud and definite voices, very good for stability. As if she should be glad. But she's not. She doesn't care about tennis, she hasn't ever hit a ball in her life — that's all in the future. And she doesn't care about stability, not at all, because this really is a long time ago, back in the middle of all our childhoods and —

And the bird swoops over the hedge into the next field and disappears. And she's only six, well six and a bit, and the sack is rough and the field is wide and green and it's making her dizzy and feel a bit like crying when she thinks of what must happen when the whistle blows.

*

Water. The idea of water is in her life already. She likes water a bit but only if it's shallow. She doesn't want water anywhere near her face. She'll have a bath and play with the toys — tipping the Matey blue bathwater in and out of the red and yellow cups — but she screams if you try and wash her hair.

One time her Mum gives her a wind-up submarine to play with in the bath and, while the girl's absorbed in letting it whirr round and round and dive under, her Mum quietly fills a bowl with water and tries to rinse her hair.

Immediately she screams and struggles and fights. She thinks she's drowning. Water sloshes out all over the bathroom floor and she is In Trouble – that means smack bottom and straight to bed.

The following week her Mum gets her a special pink plastic cap a bit like a saucer to wear on her head, so the water doesn't go in her eyes. She lets her Mum put it on and she stays brave and tense, breath held, while her Mum fills bowls and bowls of water to rinse the soap away. Johnson's Baby Shampoo. It doesn't go in her eyes, it doesn't sting and neither does the water. She can feel it on her ears and down the back of her neck and she can also feel the slow, warm weight of it in her hair, taking the shampoo away, but that's all right.

'All gone?' she says when the water has stopped running over her head.

Her Mum puts the bowl back next to the basin.

'That's right, all gone. Good girl. All gone.'

The pink plastic cap stays by the bath and she tries not to look at it every time she goes in the bathroom. She'll have her hair rinsed now but still the idea of having all that water poured over her head makes her tense right up. The sight of the pink cap overshadows her life, her days, her whole week.

*

When she is three or four, her Daddy fills a bright blue paddling pool for her – a big square expensive one, with a frame you have to screw together using tools, and proper wooden seats, made to last, on the corners. It takes a very long time to fill and you must be patient or you won't be allowed to go in. Sometimes he lets go of the hose and leaves it in so he can go and do something else while he's waiting, but she doesn't like that because it makes her think there's a snake in the water – a wiggly, sliding sea snake – and she won't get in.

Just one glimpse of the hose resting darkly down there on the bottom of the pool makes her shudder.

So to please her, he stands there on a hot day and holds the hose with both hands, cigarette between his lips, ash dropping on the patio. There's a plastic starfish, a watering can with a flower where the sprinkles come out. The air smells of roses, of tap water on hot stone.

She stands in the pool filling and pouring and refilling, hours of this. She won't sit down in it, she just likes to stand. If her Mum suggests she gets wet all over, to cool down or to have fun, she just says, I like it dry like this! and carries on playing. Her baby sister staggers in wearing a nappy, cries, has to be carried, dripping, back into the house. She is always falling into things – flower beds, swimming pools – and having to be lifted out, screaming.

*

Her Mum says that races are healthy, that everyone should learn to compete. But her Mum's different. There are pictures of her looking just as you'd imagine: tall, defiant, ready to run.

'But why? What's healthy about them?' I ask her when I am about eleven.

'It's good for people to compete.'

'But why?'

'Just generally. So they know where they stand. So you know if you are slower or faster than the rest. It's fun – to push yourself, to develop stamina, to try.'

'But I know what I am. I know I'm always going to be slow and I don't care.'

*

'You don't want a prize?'

My Mum's face is disbelieving. I'm thirteen now and I've told her I still don't care. She sets her mouth in a thin line and stares at me. It's the same mouth she uses a few years later when I tell her I can think of nothing worse than doing business studies at university.

'What, you mean a little red ribbon?'

Mum smiles.

'I can't get all worked up about a little bit of ribbon.'

'Oh come on. It's more than that. It's what it stands for.'

'What? What does it stand for?'

'For being best.'

'I don't want to be the best, I just want to be – me.'

*

But the fact is unavoidable: everyone wants to talk to the girls with the red ribbons pinned on them. Winning equals popularity. Those girls are the ones sitting up there right now on the high brick wall at breaktime eating Wagon Wheels, sandalled feet swinging.

It's a long way down but they're not scared, why should they be? Nothing scares them, there's nothing in the world they can't solve or deal with. They got up here somehow didn't they? So they'll get down. When they jump, skirts will fly up and knickers – white, red, navy – will show.

Meanwhile there they sit, cracking off the chocolate with their teeth, to get down to the white line of marshmallow underneath. They are the ones with the longest, sleekest ponytails, the ones with thin ankles and eager jaws, who sparkle and talk loudly in the dinner queue.

The fast ones are the ones who dare. The slowest

ones are the fat ones or the ones with the wrong PE kit or divorced parents or strange birthmarks that make people stare. Or the ones who are just scared of everything and would rather not have the world shift and change because of the timing of a race. This is me, this is her.

*

My Mum looks at me as if I am a mystery – as if it seems unlikely that I really came out of her, this child with the non-competitive spirit and the little pouty mouth and the big feet and scared body.

'You would think, with your body and your feet, you'd be able to run. You'd think you'd at least be willing to try.'

But no, doesn't she see this? Trying is too finite. It draws attention. What Mum doesn't see is that I've learned not to mind the ignominy of being last, in fact I don't mind it at all, I welcome it. That position, that lastness, is my friend. I've worked out that someone has to be last and it may as well be me. Save the others the grief and disappointment of failing and keep the world steady and predictable for myself.

The other day at dinner, Lucy S put her two scoops of mashed potato in the pockets of her overall and emptied it down the toilet. No one found out but now her overall pockets are mouldy and she daren't take it home to be washed or then her Mum will know. So now she has a stinking overall for the rest of term. But I understand this, Lucy's safe. Lucy got a blue ribbon in the relay. A blue is good, not as good as a red but good enough to keep you popular, especially if you do risky things like putting your dinner down the toilet.

*

Her father isn't really sporty, but he likes swimming, always has done. He says there's nothing to beat a good swim in the sea, as opposed to a pool, which is tricky as he doesn't like to leave Nottingham which is bang in the middle of England as anyone knows.

In the RAF, he swam in warm seas, deep azure oceans. He saw sea snakes, phosphorescence, dolphins with their swooping gait and friendly noses. He once saw a shark. He wasn't scared. In the South of France, the only other time he ever went abroad if you don't count the RAF, he once had the pleasure of visiting a nudist beach – Le Lavandou. You went there by boat and the people had no clothes on at all. Not just topless but completely nude. It was perfectly legal. Le Lavandou.

He pronounces the word with awe and care as if it was itself naked and exposed. She tries to imagine a nudist beach. She wonders if all the grown-ups run around giggling, the way she and her sisters do when they take their clothes off.

*

On the complicated jigsaw of the British Isles which she got for Christmas, Nottingham is in the middle, London is where the Queen is and Rutland is the tiniest, dinkiest piece that you drop on the carpet and lose if you're not careful.

She likes Rutland and she always tries to wait and put it in last.

There's sea all around the edge of the jigsaw because we are an island. You start by doing the edge then you fill in the middle. Imagine if you lived on the edge, she thinks, and you woke up and saw sea every single day – the bright sparkle of all that blue right outside your door, your window. She wonders if there are schools for children who live by the sea. She imagines not. She imagines that if you're lucky enough to live on the edge then you're always going to feel holidayish and happy and free.

*

'On your marks, get set . . .'

Mrs Rogers. Long, smooth face – smooth and young even though she's old – curly white hair, a tallness that makes her bossy but in a kind way. No one hates her but no one exactly likes her either.

On your marks, get set. Just those few words are enough to make the six-year-old girl with boy's hair feel horrible inside. Mrs Rogers has on: navy tracksuit bottoms, Aertex top like theirs (only hers is white), wristwatch (they can't wear their watches for PE), glasses with blue see-through edges. Her fingernails are short and clean and sensible, her hands always brown in an outdoors way, her mouth has never been near the slippery scarlet of a lipstick. Mrs Rogers: the whistle is around her neck. She's never angry and she doesn't shout but she is firm in a plain, calm way and you obey her. Her dog Jenny has not been allowed to come here today but she can't be left in the car either so she's stayed at home. This is a serious day and it will be over, it has to be, soon it really will, but right now I'm not going to let myself think about it.

*

Death. She remembers very well being four years old, a bright and trembly paper doll of a child, and suddenly being hit by the weight of knowing it's not all about light. That there's a big dark shadow on the world. That people don't speak out loud about it but it's there all right.

It's a black animal that lies down on your face and won't let you breathe. It's like sleep, only worse, it goes on for longer and you can't wake up because it presses down on you, cold and final.

In her nursery there is a large toy-box with a

lift-up lid. The toy-box is covered in dirty white quilted plastic, stapled and glued at the corners but peeling off so you can see some of the foam padding underneath and the yellow honey of the glue. She puts her face close up to inspect the dried drips of glue. She loves the drips. Every day she picks off a bit and puts it inside her toy purse that does up with a click. Her secret place for keeping bits of things.

Inside the toy-box are: white-haired dollies with upset faces (well so would you be upset if someone scribbled on your face with felt tip), pretend food like brown plastic turkey on a plate (sad legs sticking up in the air) and plastic grapes, and a pretend cooker with knobs that really twiddle. Also, a clown that rolls around on its plastic base that was given to her baby sister when she was born the other day. And a squirrel you wind up and it jogs along and, best of all, a rabbit made of soap. If you put the rabbit in a warm place, like by a radiator, it grows fur on its back. A chemical reaction, her father says, reaching for an ashtray to stub out his cigarette, but she doesn't care about things like reactions, she just wants to love and pat and stroke it.

If you climb onto the toy-box you can jump down. It's a game, just a game, you won't get hurt. But she's not so sure. The nursery used to be a garage so the floor is concrete under the lino, hard and cold. She stands on the toy-box and considers jumping, she wants to, she wants to play the game, she doesn't want to be left out. But a part of her knows that if she does it, if she lets herself do it and lets herself go, then all her bones will break in half and she will die.

Death is the dark shadow peeling its slow way over the world.

If you are dead you go underground and lie in darkness for ever. Even if you believe in Jesus, this still happens, only if you believe in Him, there might be a Shining Light to Guide you Through. (Her Grandpa told her this but they're not really allowed to spend much time with him because he just slides off into madness and says, Hallelujah Praise the Lord! all the time with his arm in the air.) And if all her bones were broken they'd even have trouble fitting her in the box, it would have to be a different-shaped box, not a normal coffin but like a big version of a grocery box. Crammed in and sealed up with tape. To lie in darkness for ever, your bones curled and tight. The thought is a panic thought and she has to almost stop breathing just to get rid of it. Tearing at a nail with her teeth helps calm her down.

She doesn't do it – she doesn't jump. She is four years old and this is the real beginning of her relationship with sport. There's no picture of this in the family album. There is no one there to record it and even if there was, this would not be the picture they'd choose to take. The pictures in the album are always what you did, never what you didn't dare do.

*

She likes dancing. It's different from PE because no one wins, no one judges, though Mrs Varten is actually stricter and crosser than any games teacher at school.

'Tails in, stomachs in,' says Mrs Varten. She says you should imagine you're a puppet with a string coming out of your head. She thinks of the gypsy puppet her sister got from Hamleys in London. Round pink shiny face, black fuzzy hair, red skirt with a zigzag of green nylon ribbon around the edge. But puppets are the least graceful people she knows. They jerk and then when you stop moving them they lie flat and dead. She wants to be like the doll on the musical box – tall, perfect, arms outstretched, standing on her toes.

She looks down at her feet, flat small feet in pale pink leather ballet shoes held on with an elastic sewn across by her Mum. Mrs Varten doesn't wear ballet shoes at all, but black leather shoes with a heel and a strap fastened by a little leather button. They are called character shoes. Mrs Varten is a character, her Mum says. When grown-ups say that about someone it usually means they don't like them.

After the curtseys they all sit in a row on the cold stone steps and hold their hands out and Smarties are put into them – tipped from a white tube, two or three each. They sit and crunch. Not good for your teeth but who cares about teeth when dancing is all about toes?

*

My parents got married in August. They'd only known each other a few months. His car broke down and he stopped off and asked to use the phone in her father's – my grandfather's – office and he saw her sitting there and asked her out On The Spot. She said yes, maybe partly because his car was a sports car, a sleek blue creature that knew how to go fast, whereas he was always slow, slow and misunderstood he said. Where did they go? To the pictures, to a milk bar, to a restaurant? My father didn't like restaurants and he didn't like going out, or talking. Over the next fourteen years my mother grew louder and more frantic, for lack of anyone replying.

But he managed to ask her to marry him and she said, Yes. Later he wrote and asked if she'd got cold feet and she said, No, not at all, she loved him and they would go ahead with it. And anyway she couldn't bear living with her own father any more.

She swapped a religious man for a man who didn't believe in anything. They had a wedding cake with two people standing on the top of it. He was thirty-two and a bachelor and she was twenty and wore gingham and for their honeymoon they went on an aeroplane to Nice. Then home to a small house with polished floors and his mother living in it.

*

I hate this day and I hate being in this sack, but I have no choice. Children have no choice because this is school and if they put you in a sack you have to stay in it, that's what school's about: doing all the things you don't want to do.

'It was exactly the same in my day,' my Daddy says, smiling at his own face in the mirror and rubbing the sides of his thin black hair with Brylcreem. 'You think we enjoyed school?'

Because school is character-building, my Mum always says, it's where they make you Be A Sport and Join In and, though they make you do that several times a week, once a year they make you do it with equipment and organised lines and the awfulness of an audience: Sports Day.

I hate and dread it so I must need to have my character built.

If I was religious I would pray to God to just somehow get me out of here (Get me out of this sack God!) but my family don't believe in Him unless you count my grandfather who is mad and not really allowed at our house except once at Christmas and then never again.

My father thinks people who believe in Him are lunatics, stark raving mad. If God is so effective, my father likes to say, then why is there so much suffering in the world? Why are there wars? And death? Why did both your goldfish die in the course of the same weekend? Explain that.

*

In the Air Force, Daddy says, it got so hot you could fry an egg on the wing of a plane. Burma, Singapore, Malaysia. Bananas and natives, huge trees with oval leaves, huge hot skies, rainy seasons, roofs made of straw. There are photos of him smoking in these places with no shirt on, you can see the round dark splodges of his nipples. In one he is holding up a bunch of bananas and laughing at them – to prove he has seen them, to show he is there. That's why you take photos, to show where you've been. Hot, surprising places I never went, I've still never been. Scalding hot metal. Lacy egg white, sunshine yolk – I always stab mine with a fork because it's satisfying, to show it's mine.

He went to all those places but he still preferred Nottingham. He didn't believe in travel, not really, just as he didn't believe in God. All those punctured yolks. All those men away from home with no shirts on and their nipples showing and stabbing their fried eggs all over the wide, exotic world and dreaming of home.

*

It's a hot day and Mummy has yellow roses to go in a vase in the hall.

'You're working hard today,' she says to me, 'delivering your milk.'

'Yes,' I say, blowing air out the way I've seen my Daddy do when he comes in the hall and puts his keys down after the factory. 'It's a very hard day actually. Actually I think I'll have a sleep in a minute.'

That's my new word: actually.

'Oh,' she says, 'but before you do – you know, I think I've changed my mind. I asked for three pints but I do believe I'd like four.'

I think about this.

'Two more?'

'No,' she says. 'Just one. Three and one make four.'

I put out my fingers to help think about this. I am four. That's two and two. I go to my lorry and pull it to the step.

'How many did you say?'

'Look,' says my Mum, 'I'll show you' – and she kneels down gently on the step and she pulls out the bottles and shows me how to count them. She has brown hair and she smells of bathroom and talcum powder. This is my happiest time, counting out the milk with my powdery Mum.

'Soon,' she says, in the same whispery voice, 'you'll go to school. Then you'll know all the numbers up to a hundred – think of that.'

I go stiff. I don't want to think of that.

'I don't need to go to school, you know.'

'Of course you do my love.'

'I don't want to know up to a hundred,' I tell her, 'I only want to know this many. I only have this much milk bottles in my lorry.'

She laughs.

'Ten,' she says. 'You have ten. You'll have other children to play with at school. You'll have such fun.'

'I don't want fun.'

She smiles to herself, as if she hasn't heard me, as if she isn't my Mum.

'No,' I say as she straightens up, unties her apron, moves away, 'I just want to be with you.'

In my mind the other children are running towards me with their big faces and big hands and their fun and I am running the other way.

Mummy smiles. Her apron has pictures of fruit on it. A pineapple, a bunch of cherries. Her other apron is a picture of a piece of cake. She hangs the apron on the hook on the back of the kitchen door.

I take a breath.

I want to carry on explaining but instead I hear myself start to cry. I'm not sure if the crying is inside or outside but my Mum either doesn't notice or pretends not to. She thinks it's best to ignore me. She turns away and makes a noise running the tap to fill the rose vase to put the yellow roses in.

*

I have a beret for school and a satchel and a red pleated skirt. I've never had anything with pleats before. Pleats are grown-up. Smart brown Start-Rite shoes and fuzzy pale brown socks that itch my legs. My Mum says all these clothes are terribly exciting when she lays them on the bed with their name-tapes freshly sewn on, but when she sees me actually standing in them she has tears running down from her eyes.

It's a bright September morning, a day like all the other days but different. It lies in wait for me. Daddy takes a photograph of me standing by the front door, blinking and holding on tight to its edge. I look like a big girl, he says, and it's true, when I look in the mirror I see that I do. I look like a real person, a smaller version of a proper grown-up. Not like my sister who still puts Weetabix in her hair or tips it on the floor if you give her a bowl to manage on her own.

'I don't want to go to school.'

'You'll be all right when you get there.'

'I've got tummy-ache.'

'It'll go once you're there, you'll see.'

'What if it doesn't?'

'It will, trust me, it will.'

I also have a different skirt that fastens at the side. It goes in a soft bag with an Aertex shirt. The skirt is stiff and has a hook. It's a Big Girl fastening.

'What's this for?' I ask with increasing suspicion.

'That's for games. It's your games skirt.'

'Why do I need a special skirt to play games?'

'Because these are special games. It's running around. It's PE.'

'I don't want to run around.'

'Oh Julie, now you're being silly.'

'I don't want to!'

'You will. You'll want to when you see all the other children.'

'I don't like other children.'

This is true. The only other children I know are my two baby sisters and they never do anything bad except sleep and cry and that's not my fault. In fact really they aren't children at all, babies aren't. They're not much different from our goldfish in the bowl, or the cat next door. I don't want anything more challenging than this in my life and that's the truth.

'You can't know, you've never met them.'

'And what if I can't do it up?'

'The skirt? Well, someone will help you. You must remember to ask if you need help.'

I start to cry.

'I don't want to play games in a skirt. I want to do pictures and listen to stories.'

'You'll do both of those things, sweetheart.'

*

Daddy takes me up the hill to school. The dark, dark hill which trembles and tilts as we walk. Everything is giant, everything threatens. Outside it's sunny with light flickering in the trees, but in the school it's dark and weepy, the air thick with parents leaving children, tiptoeing away with too bright voices, pretending it's normal when we know it's not.

If parents lie to you, they only do it to help you. White lies, to make you brave, to make you believe the world is safe when it's not.

As Daddy begins to go I feel my eyes get wet so to stop the tears I close my eyes, but I bang into another child. When I open them again Daddy is gone and there's a sick, bad space where his back was. I don't cry, I just stand there and shake.

*

'And if He's so Almighty,' her father says, 'why doesn't He just pick the winner of the Grand National and make Himself a fortune? Why doesn't he do the Pools or Spot the Ball? I know I jolly well would, if I had that kind of power.'

'But Daddy, God doesn't care about being rich. God is above money.'

'Nothing to stop Him giving His winnings away to the poor and needy though, is there? Ha! Give the poor blighters a cash incentive to come to church, that would pack 'em in.'

'But Daddy —'

But it's no use. Daddy doesn't realise that if God exists — and I'm not saying He does, I'm just saying what they tell us at school — He's going to think along slightly different lines from ordinary people.

Daddy hasn't come to Sports Day, because it's a weekday and he's at his factory. On weekdays he uses his Valet Chair and his Trouser Press, but on Saturday and Sunday he Lies In with his Teasmade. Then he takes us swimming, reads the News of the World while we scream for forty minutes in the water. Sometimes he comes in too. Careful breaststroke lengths before Sunday lunch. Rest of the time he's either at his factory or driving to or from it in his car which is racing green and smells of cigarillos which are healthier than cigarettes, though he smokes those too.

Daddy hated school because they hit him all the time, but it was much more normal to beat people in those days. He left at fifteen even though he was a bright boy, verging on genius, he admits, when it came to inventing. Luckily you didn't need school to learn vacuum forming and injection moulding, which is his real job. He owns the whole of his factory, which is two big rooms. At this school they don't beat you, but that's partly because these are modern days and partly because we're all girls. It's a girls' school. If you want to hurt girls, you just put them in a sack and make them jump.

Oh look, the bird is back. A small brown bird with a sharp spiky tail. There are two birds now, diving against each other like pencil drawings scribbled over the sky. It's so hot today, fidgety hot, clouds of small flies lifting and dropping over everyone's heads.

Here I am, then, in a hot rough sack with my plimsolled feet down the bottom and my small bitten fingers holding the rough edge of the top. Black words that I can't read printed on it. Or I could read them if I wanted (because I can read, I learned when I was four) but they're upside down and anyway I'm not interested. Hate the sack, hate the hot hairy feel of being in it. It's a long time ago but not so many years that I don't remember — that sack, that field, that hairiness, that heat, burnt on my brain, my memory. The pain of it burnt on. Six years old, the sky bright with heat, the birds disappearing together over the hedge.

*

When she is five he builds a swimming pool in their house – a real one, actually there in their house right next to the sitting room – an indoor swimming pool.

Their friends are jealous. It's all the rage. Her father likes it because it means he can swim in the nude, just like at Le Lavandou. South of France comes to Mapperley Park. But she hates it — because she is afraid of her nose filling up and water on her face and sea snakes and drowning and because she can see all the dark gristle and hair of him drifting and moving under the water.

*

Every time you run, every time you win or you lose, the world changes around you, shifts its position slightly and you are either in front or behind but either way you're not where you were before, never where you were. This feeling, this possibility, makes her sick and dizzy. More than anything, she likes things to stay the same.

And the field is green, the grassy crayoned green of a field in a book. It's not the field I mind, I like the field. If I were a grown-up and could do what I liked (like wear high heels all day like Mummy or buy a sweetshop and just eat all the sweets in it) I would sit down right here and pull up the grass and maybe pick a mauve clover and suck the honey out and count the leaves looking for a lucky one with four and let ladybirds run races over the top of my little finger and think about later when it's all over and I can go home. Except if I was a grown-up I suppose I could just get up and go home whenever I liked.

'Make your way calmly and quietly to the car park where your parents will collect you from your form teacher.'

It's hot, too hot and lines are marked on the grass in white — lines which you can easily see from far away but which, when you get up close, hardly seem to be lines at all, just a mess of white on the surface of the world. How it must look to an insect.

Look down and it looks like each separate sticky blade of grass has been individually licked with white paint. But put your face right down close and you can see that some parts of the grass have been missed, while some actual crumbs of soil have been painted. You hope a flower or a ladybird did not get painted by mistake. Would they struggle along, slowly dying from the poisonous weight of the paint? It seems too cruel to do that to a small insect, just so a school can have lines for its Sports Day.

Mr Jones did them yesterday with a metal wheel you push along, we saw him doing them when we came up here for practice and he waved to us, he was smoking a cigarette and he put it in his mouth so he could wave with one hand while pushing the wheel along with the other. Mr Jones is the caretaker. He can't know about the insects. He wouldn't harm a fly. His nose is a little bit purple and a bit big, somehow the wrong colour and the wrong size for his face, and his skin has lots of worrying little holes in it, but it's a kind face. If this was a story, he would be a goody not a baddy. He does all the odd jobs, all the difficult and dirty ones no one else wants to do. Sometimes he has to go in the girls' toilets to fix things but he always announces himself first by calling out, so you can pull up your knickers and he doesn't make you jump.

*

The armbands smell of new hot plastic. That's because the sun's been beating down on the basket they live in. Poor armbands. She imagines them waiting in their basket all happy and warm and wishing and wishing no one would take them out and blow them up and make them go in the pool.

The Sun Room, my Mum calls this room. The windows are huge and everything in it is basket this and basket that. It has a Basket Chair which she sits in to put on my armbands and a basket table with an ashtray on it, a heavy gold glass one with bubbles trapped in the glass. I don't like the feeling of the air coming in and the way they tighten on my arms. I feel all puffed up, like a creature with false wings. Except I can't fly or swim, not now, not ever, I can't even move.

I am naked except for armbands. I jump up and down in pure naked terror.

'Come on, darling, come on in,' says Mum, holding out her arms in a coaxing way. 'The water's lovely. It's lovely in here.'

'No!'

I try to fold my arms but the armbands stop me. They are furious.

'They want to go back in their basket,' I tell my Mum.

'What?'

'The armbands want to be in the basket.'

She looks baffled, tries holding out her arms again.

'You have to learn to swim, darling. At this rate the girls will be swimming before you.'

'I don't care.'

'Swimming's really important.'

'I'll learn, I will! When I'm older.'

'That may be too late.'

They knew a boy who drowned. He drowned just before Christmas in a lake a long way away, at least eight miles. A lake in a gravel pit. An artificial lake. He drowned in an artificial lake. She thinks about the sad stupidness of this – that he drowned before Christmas, before he could have the excitement of opening his presents, and he didn't even drown in a real lake. It's like a joke, except it isn't because he's dead.

She thinks a lot about the boy even though she doesn't remember his face or name, is not even sure she really knew him. She imagines his skeleton floating to the top. She hates the smell of chlorine, the light patterns the blue water makes on the ceiling. She hates everything to do with water and swimming and pools.

When she is nine, her father takes her and her sisters to the local pool – Bingham or Southwell. Bingham is big and booming, full of rough boys.

Southwell is smaller with more light coming in. Both have a chocolate machine with Dairy Crunch in.

He takes longer to get ready than they do but soon he emerges from the Male Changing. He isn't in the nude. He wears drab brown trunks with a white cord to do them up. He has a bald patch where his hair's wearing out. He waves to them and dives in, the water smacks against the length of him. Then he surfaces, wipes back his hair, snorts grey snot out of his nose and pushes off from the end of the pool and swims lengths and lengths of breaststroke. Calm, endless lengths. He is the only man she knows who only does breaststroke, never crawl. She thinks it's maybe because he likes the word breast. That too reminds him of the South of France.

*

This is her — the child you saw just now, a brown-haired girl in a sack — and it's about two minutes ago and she's sniffing the air that smells of grass and seed and buttercup heads and screwing her eyes up in the itchy bright summer light and blinking away the beginnings of tears. Her Mum is there waving and waving and she wants to run, but not in the way everyone wants her to. Not in a healthy competition sort of way but in a running-away way. Not half jump half stagger in a sack to the end of the race but get out of there fast, before any of it can happen.

Her Mum's eyes find her in the crowd and she waves brightly at her daughter and the daughter waves brightly back and then, holding all her breath in her chest and in fact not really breathing at all, she automatically puts the tip of her third left finger in her mouth. Tearing at the flesh with her teeth comforts her, calms her down. But her Mum makes a frowny face and points at the child's finger and straightaway without a flicker of resistance in her face she removes it and closes her mouth. She didn't realise she'd stopped breathing. Sometimes a moment without breath is a quick, harsh comfort to her.

*

Here is a cine-film taken by Daddy of me at my very first Sports Day: the Wyvil School, Nottingham, July 1965. Miss Hancock, who is old and big with white hair, is the headmistress and Miss Betty, who is old and little with grey hair, is her younger sister, the deputy.

Deputy Dawg is a character on TV.

'Just like you have little sisters,' Miss Hancock tells me, 'I have a little sister too: Miss Betty, ha, ha!'

The girl who is trying to be me doesn't laugh, she just stands there, forlorn and pale and shaky and with tummy-ache. She hates it when teachers try to talk to her. She prefers it when they are far away where they should be – taking Assembly, at the front of the class. She still hates school but she goes every day, every single day of her poor small life, except for weekends. She's got used to waking every day with a hot sharp pain in her stomach. Except for Saturday. Saturday is a good day, a gold-coloured free day when she doesn't think about it. But the pretend whiteness of Sunday is lived under the cold dark shadow of Monday, the blueness of school.

This is a fact, the way it is. She's five and a half and fear has become a routine part of her life.

*

Miss Hancock has the exact same birthday as me — 2 June. I'm five, she's about a hundred, she's probably always been a hundred, I don't really in my heart think she ever can have been a real, live child.

Soon she'll die. That's worse, far worse, than having Monday hanging over you. The darkness of the grave. But she won't die now, not today, not on her birthday. You only die on your birthday if God hates you. On that day, when my father brings me into the narrow, dark hall, she beckons me into her study and gives me a present, a small ivory elephant, delicate as a bone and creamy white.

'Because you're my twin,' she says, giggling in a silly ungrown-up way.

I wonder how I can be twins with someone like her. She's kind but her bosoms hang right down to her knees and I'm not joking. She is nice unless you're rude or answer back, then she smacks you with a ruler hard enough to make a red mark. She has the big brown study that smells of cat, with the sofa and the armchairs and the teacups with horrid brown stains on them and Miss Betty has a little room off to the side which smells of nothing and looks like no one's ever really dared go in.

For my birthday I had a card from Mummy and Daddy with real glitter all over it. For our Princess! it said and there was a girl's face with a surprised look and lashes drawn around her eyes.

If you're late for school and prayers have started, then you'll walk past the two rooms and see the doors wide open and no one in there. A finished tea tray on the table, an umbrella rolled up in the corner. The sound of hymns from the Hall, the terrible fact of all those voices blending and you excluded, the terrible terror of having to wait in the vestibule to be told off and hit with a ruler. Not hard but enough to make you flinch and have the hot wet start of tears in your eyes.

*

The two sisters are so old they have to sit down for

Sports Day. Two antique upholstered chairs are carried onto the lawn by the caretaker, Mr Fishwick, who always has a bit of dirt on his trousers. The chairs almost match the flower beds and they look all funny and homely because they're not really outside chairs.

The sisters sit smiling, wearing dark sun flaps over their glasses. They look like insects or animals. Miss Hancock holds her walking stick out in front of her, Miss Betty doesn't need one as she's younger.

Even though it's piercingly hot, Miss Hancock wears a thick wool cardigan, flat leather shoes with holes punched in. Miss Betty has a hat tied under her chin. The sun beats down on the flowers on the rockery, red, yellow, orange, mauve – snapdragons and wallflowers – and the mothers wear frocks and smile and clap, one hand cupped over their eyes so they can find their sons or daughters. Tieless fathers hold cameras, smoke cigarettes, flicking the ash on the flower beds. Miss Betty comes over and politely asks them to be careful of the flowers. One of them, one of the Dads, says something back to her and you can tell it's something friendly because she listens, tips her head to one side and sort of laughs. Then she tiptoes back to her seat.

This all takes place in black and white and in slow motion, on a hot and faraway day in the 1960s.

At first you can't see me anywhere, but then the camera finds me. The camera is my father and he doesn't give up until he finds me, the star of this home movie. There's a juddery moment of waving around and focusing. Then there I clearly am, smallest girl in a crowd of small girls, short dark hair with a gingham bow topknot, a sash around my chest and a games skirt on, done up with a hook, no idea why I'm there, here I am standing and twisting around, finger in my mouth as always, eyes tight and dark.

I look about five – incredibly anxious, incredibly distressed.

*

Behind me, not noticing me at all, a young, brown-haired teacher with a slim waist, long legs and pointy breasts, blows on her whistle and smiles and points and walks and gives orders. Shorts like a man's shorts, Aertex shirt, plimsolls, a gold watch slipping over her slim wrist, wedding ring glinting in the sun.

'Can we have everyone for the egg and spoon over here at the double please!'

Mrs Hannah – shoulders back, stomach in, head tall – caught on film on a hot day in 1965. She tosses her head and looks beadily back and forth, checking along the lines of children, checking her watch. She seems old then – certainly older than my Mummy, which means she may be as much as twenty-seven.

'Lower Prep, where are your ribbons?'

She is in charge of Sports Day, she's running the whole show. Miss Hancock and Miss Betty watch in a daze. They haven't attempted a Sports Day before, unless you count the silly day they had last June in the small Hall when it was wet outside. But that came to nothing. No one managed to win anything for goodness' sake! At last this feels proper. At last someone who knows about races. Silently they congratulate themselves on their wise appointment. They'll make sure Nansi does it next year, and the next.

Mrs Hannah pauses, whistle between her lips.

'They're where? Well why? Yes, fetch them now! Of course now – go on do it, fast!'

She marches down the line and gathers up cones, then scatters small red, blue and green beanbags across the course. Why? Who cares? Because when she moves she does it with such incredible, plausible briskness that even the parents are in awe. Doctors, solicitors, clerks, housewives all shuffle and jump and scatter out of her way.

*

And the sky – the sky is perfect hot blue, nothing in it at all but sky — no clouds, no birds. Blue emptiness of sky, makes you think of holidays.

'Lovely Sports Day weather!' declared my Mum happily this morning as she put my Cracker Barrel cheese sandwiches in a bag and made me take a hat.

She made her voice cheerful because she knows I don't like Sports Day and it was her way of encouraging me, but it was also her way of saying, Don't tell me you feel too ill to go to school because I won't believe you.

Here on the field, they give us barley water in scratched plastic cups borrowed from Lower Prep paint room and the taste of it makes me think of the dim worry of going to play at other people's houses and somewhere far away there's the drone of a tractor, drowned out only by parents' cheers, the long note of a whistle, a teacher with a thing you talk into.

*

Grandfather is not allowed in our house because of being a religious maniac, but we're allowed to see him at Granny's. Or at least, our parents aren't that keen about us seeing him at all but when Granny has us over after school sometimes or quite often he's there and as Mummy reminds Daddy, 'What can you do about it? It's his house and he has every right to be there and what's more I rely on my mother to have the children.'

Because Granny and Grandfather used to have a

café down by the River Trent (where they sold Wall's
ice cream which Daddy always says is nothing like
as good as Lyons Maid), Granny can make doughnuts, home-made ones from scratch. They are
completely different from bought ones – they are
crunchy and they taste of sugar and frying. First she
makes the dough, then she fries it and dips them
in the sugar, then shakes them in the tea towel to
get the sugar off, then tips them on a plate and you
eat them still warmly oozing jam.

But you have to wait while she does them. Usually
she sings while she kneads the dough – hymns or
snatches of theme tunes off the TV. *Peyton Place* or *The
Persuaders*. She's religious but not in the same way as
Grandfather. She believes in God but much more
gently and quietly and she goes to a proper normal
church where there are other people who do baking
and help others, whereas Grandfather has been
thrown out of seven whole churches and even they
weren't proper ones!

That's because he thinks he is the Chosen One,
she told us one day, laughing so much she could
hardly breathe and she had to get her hanky out to
wipe the tears that trickled down.

Grandfather thinks television and women with
short hair are the work of the Devil. As well as being
a Believer, he is also a Collector. He collects old bird

baths and typewriters and violins and recently he's started collecting old Coke cans. He keeps them all stacked up in the bath which means that Granny can't have a bath any more, she has to use the shower instead. For a while, his bedroom was so full of typewriters and bird baths that he had to sleep in a caravan outside in the street, but he's got rid of most of them and he's moved back in now. Granny says she almost preferred it when he was in the caravan, but she says it like she says most things, half laughing and half crying and as if she doesn't really dare mean it.

Sometimes while we wait for the doughnuts Grandfather is out, giving out tracts about The Word to people in the street or else pinning them to the trees in Woodthorpe Park, where the park keeper straightaway rips them down. But if he's at home, he takes the opportunity of us being trapped waiting for doughnuts to talk to us about The Word and The Good News and Our Saviour Jesus Christ. Sometimes we listen and sometimes we don't but we're used to it by now and so we're not scared, not really, we know that even when he shouts he doesn't mean any real harm.

We won't tell Mum though because she might not let us come any more and that would be the end of the doughnuts.

'Well,' says Grandfather to my littlest sister D. 'And what have you been doing at school today?'

'Nothing.'

She wipes her milk moustache on her sleeve.

Grandfather puts his hands in his jacket pockets and looks at her. When he moves his arms you can smell the sweat seeping out of the lining of his jacket.

'Nothing?'

'Mmmm. Nothing.'

'Oh really? Why is that then?'

D sighs.

'Because it's Sports Day. Tomorrow. We had to practise.'

Straightaway Grandfather looks happy. He sees an opening.

'Ah! That's very important, Sports Day is! You must win, you must be sure to win!'

His spit flies out of his mouth and lands on some papers on a chair. We all blink.

My other sister, M, giggles.

'It's not the winning,' she says primly, 'it's the taking part that counts.'

For a moment Grandfather looks muddled and this makes him look strange, maybe because he's such a big man, with thick white hair and strong tall legs, not at all like an old man really, not old the way Granny is old and sweet and a bit tired. Grandfather bounds around, more like a child than a man. Now he licks his lips.

'Shall I give you a tip about Sports Day?'

D shrugs. She doesn't really care. She's hungry. I look at M, who looks at me and rolls her eyes.

He licks his lips again and spreads his fingers.

'Fix your eyes on Jesus. I mean it! Paul runs a marathon in Corinthians, you can look it up yourself: Chapter 9, Verses 24 and 25. It's right there in the Bible if you don't believe me and you see what's more because he was on the Lord's Business he was determined to win, taking part was not enough, no sitting around for him . . . Oh no!'

'Eric!' Granny calls from the sizzling kitchen, 'I hope you're not preaching to those children?'

Straightaway Grandfather alters his voice.

'Calm down Emilia,' he says, and he knows she can't come in and rescue us because it's dangerous to leave a pan of hot fat. 'We're just having a nice chat about school, aren't we?'

He leans forward to us and lowers his voice, flicks a glance in the direction of the kitchen.

'Life is not a spectator sport,' he says, mostly to my sisters. 'Fix your eyes on Jesus, that's the trick, amen, yes.'

His voice has snaked right down to a breathy hiss as he adds, 'Hallelujah Praise the Lord!'

*

Paul in Corinthians may have been on the Lord's Business but I am not and I would much rather sit and watch the ants marching up and over my finger-ends than run marathons. Or do heats for races. I am on Nobody's Business and if they would only leave us alone we could make a hideaway out of overalls in the corner of the playground and imagine we are something and somewhere else.

*

The heats. Ten rough sacks are thrown down on the playground asphalt. Ten spoons and ten wooden cubes for eggs. Batons for the relay. I feel sick. Why do there have to be heats? Why can't we just do quiet reading?

People are talking. Diana and Celia are talking. So are others. Mrs Rogers waits for everyone to be quiet. She holds her whistle between her teeth and looks from face to face, waiting. She looks like a wolf about to pounce. No one sees her except me. People just carry on talking and then someone gets nudged and the silence hurries down the line.

'When you're ready,' Mrs Rogers says as if she means it.

But she doesn't. Her eyes shoot from side to side like wolf eyes, ready for an excuse. Then, carefully, her lips go round the whistle, she blows it hard so everyone jumps. I jump. I saw her about to blow it but I still jump.

I won't be picked. I don't want to be picked.

*

If she loses sight of her Dad in the pool and doesn't know which man of the many faceless, faraway slicked-down men he is, all she has to do is look for the bald patch and there he is.

Anyway she can swim now. One day when she is eight or maybe nine, she just gets bored and lets go of the side and doesn't go under.

'Darling!' says her Mum who had given up years ago.

She carries on. She coughs but she does not scream. She spits out the water that goes in her mouth and her feet stay off the bottom and she uses her arms to wave herself forward and she can feel the weight of the water safely under her and not on top of her and she can feel it, she can just feel it, she knows she's swimming. She is swimming, she can tell she is and it isn't at all like being a cold wet slippery fish as she's imagined but much more like being a bird – a floaty butterfly bird in motion flying through the water. A bright, slick, clever bird. Her life is altered fantastically and for ever.

'Come on, Jules, come on,' mutters her Dad.

She does a width, all the way across without putting her feet down once. When her face dips under a bit she just gulps some air and spits the water out again. Gulp and spit – her breath is harsh on her throat but she feels intensely happy and she gets to the other side, all around her people are watching and smiling and her Dad is clapping and her Mum is nearly crying.

She gets Two Pounds (two pounds!). She buys a plastic dolly in a cellophane bag from the newsagent. She has loved this dolly for a very long time and she's been there so long waiting to be bought in the window that, even through the cellophane, her dress has faded from red to pink but she doesn't mind, she doesn't want a new brighter one from the back, she only wants this one, the special faded one – the one she won with the swimming money.

*

Now she can do ten lengths. She can swim on and on and she can't remember what it was like to not be able to swim, to need armbands, to be afraid. She can even dive in. If she does a perfect dive with her head down the water stays quiet around her. She comes up quickly though, she doesn't like the deep end, but she doesn't think about it. She's learned that almost anything is possible – even diving in head first which felt like dying the first time she went down into the black water like that – as long as you don't allow yourself to think about it.

*

On holiday in Suffolk there are two small lakes, one salt water, one fresh water. Beyond them, the dunes and then the cold, crashing grey North Sea. She hates the sea – the deep chill of the water and the way the shingle dips down suddenly so you are flung out of your depth. She hates the churning brown water and the waves that come up behind you when you aren't expecting them. One time her littlest sister got pushed under by a wave and their Dad had to grab her out of the water and she was under for seconds and seconds but she came up laughing. How brave or stupid is that? She hates the whole big dangerousness of the sea out there, but she hates the two lakes more. She eyes the pale brown water with the weeds drifting around the edge and she shudders. What's under there?

Their father offers five pounds to anyone who can swim right across the salt lake. She is ten and her sisters are eight and six. It's a lot of money. Both her sisters agree immediately to do it and they put on armbands and jump straight in and there they go struggling across, breathing and splashing. They reach the opposite shore and they get the money.

'Julie?'

She shakes her head, she won't do it, she won't go in that deep unknown lake. She doesn't want the money, doesn't care about it, all she wants is to be safe, to go on living.

And she watches them have the fun of spending that money that afternoon in the town and she really doesn't mind, it's fine, it really is. She thinks her sisters are mad. She thinks they can only see the present moment, the reward, the fun. But she can see the future. And she would gladly pay not to risk herself in that black, black water.

*

Mrs Hannah lives in Woodthorpe, an area of Nottingham with a park and plenty of hairdressers, bus stops and laundrettes, in a house where the lawn stretches out beneath the terrace, green grass mown in perfect fuzzy stripes. The hall is dark and panelled, big staircase, creaking parquet floor – a house for tennis parties and cocktails and dancing. Smell of polish and coffee.

Mrs Hannah looks nothing like the eighty she claims to be – the eighty I guess she simply has to be if she taught me PE and Scottish dancing when

I was so small. This is because teachers are always old. And because they are always old, they don't age. Though I haven't set eyes on Mrs Hannah in thirty years, she looks just the same, just exactly as she's supposed to look. Strict, eager, curious, worrying.

I realise that all these years what I've carried in my head is not so much an immaculate visual image as a sensation: of a smart, slim, brown-haired female person who makes me apprehensive, sends an automatic ripple of dread through me. Rather like Mrs Rogers, no one hates her, but neither does anyone especially want to be around her. We don't like what we know she will make us do. You'd have to be mad. Who wants, after all, on a chilly black autumn morning, to undress down to vest and pants and sit shuddering and goose-pimpled on a cold gym floor?

'Repetitions, arms nicely out, tails in – all right? After me! And –'

The piano plays. And twenty-nine chilly girls hold out their arms.

*

Those eyes. If I'd never seen them again, I'd never have given them another thought, but now they're in front of me, well, I know I know those eyes. Brown with little gold flecks, slightly, briefly amused.

'Julie – hello!'

She opens the door to me and there they are, the eyes. All these years I could never have recalled them, but now I see them, I know I exactly remember them.

After the Wyvil, Mrs Hannah taught me games and dance – physical fitness – at the High School. On the phone she said she remembered me from the High School.

'Really?' This seemed highly unlikely to me.

'You had sisters in the school, yes?'

'That's right. I did.'

'Well then. I remember you. Julie Pike. I remember you.'

In Mrs Hannah's house a man is going up the stairs. He waves to me in a friendly way but Mrs Hannah shoos him on up before she lets me in the hall.

'My husband.'

'Did you drive here?' she demands to know before I can even shake her hand.

I tell her I came by train, after all.

'You naughty girl! I told you I'd pick you up if you came by train. Now then, did you eat breakfast?'

*

Her only friend is in the race, too. She and Jane made it through the heats though that's a joke as only the losers go in the sack race. Relay is for serious runners and three-legged is for people who are popular and have friends.

She and Jane got disqualified from three-legged because the purse belt they did up around their legs came loose and they both fell over and banged their heads against each other. Mrs Rogers blew her whistle and said they were Very Silly Girls Indeed and would have to do sack instead. Not even egg and spoon but sack.

Jane has red eyes because of hay fever but she isn't excused. Her freckles are so dark they're almost black. They made friends on the second day of Upper Prep and they're best pals Jane says. Pals is a word she'd never heard till Jane used it. Jane lives in Chilwell, at least eight miles by car. Now look here she is climbing into her sack. The girl watches Jane and also climbs into hers.

Jane likes Laurel and Hardy and this girl has never heard of them before she stays the night at Jane's house — her first night ever away from home. Do you like Laurel and Hardy? Jane says and she goes red because she hasn't a clue. But she says, Yes OK, and so they watch them on TV, these old black-and-white men, she can't see what's funny but she laughs.

After tea she feels a little bit sick, a bit homesick, a bit like she might have a temperature, but she puts on her baby-doll pyjamas specially bought for the occasion. White cotton with orange and pink and mauve spots on. Now they're baggy on her small seven-year-old body but she loves them so much that she's still wearing them a whole five years later when she's a long-limbed twelve-year-old, faded and stretched and washed out, but that's how special

they are to her. Jane's Mum says, How Pretty. Jane's Mum is called
Bobby like a dog or a bear in a comic. She uses words like Pal, just
as Jane does. Jane's Dad's Out At The Office and after that he'll go
Out To The Pub with some of his Pals.

She and Jane do Play-Doh in the shed which has a piece of
dirty old carpet on the floor so it feels just like a house and
there's a plastic machine that makes Play-Doh spaghetti, biscuits
for dolls. You wind the handle and it comes out, makes her think
slightly of poo but she tries not to — the long blue sausage that
you slice up with a little yellow plastic knife.

She wishes she was right there in that shed now, cutting soft
buttery-blue shapes, instead of being forced into a race she doesn't
understand.

*

'Yes,' I lie in response to Mrs Hannah's question,
hoping it's the right answer.

Because I have, at least in theory, eaten breakfast.
I always make my kids eat breakfast, everyone knows
that everyone should eat breakfast. I do approve of
breakfast, I wouldn't dream of missing it, it's just —
I didn't have much time this morning.

'Hmm.' She screws up her eyes and assesses me.
'Well, I think I'll bring some of my shortbread in
anyway.'

She carries in the tray and shuts the sitting-room
door firmly with a foot.

'To keep him out,' she explains with a wink and adds, 'He knows you're a writer. If he comes in he won't stop talking and we'll never get rid of him.'

Outside on the lawn is a creamy white magnolia, a huge candelabra, arms open to the sky. Mrs Hannah looks up from the silver coffee pot and sees me noticing it.

'Isn't it lovely?' I say.

'Oh! You know what? Funnily enough that used to be at the Wyvil. When they demolished the school in the sixties, we saved it. It was very poorly the first year and we thought we were going to lose it, but then it turned itself around the way plants often do and it came through. Look at it now, what a winner, eh?'

*

Mrs Hannah pours more coffee and offers the biscuits. I say what nice coffee it is.

'Real coffee,' she nods. 'I always have real coffee.'

I tell her I don't really like instant and she tuts approval.

'Instant! I mean, what's the point?'

She pushes the biscuit plate towards me. I took a shortbread last time, eating it with my fingers cupped to catch the crumbs. Now I take a bourbon which looks sturdier. I put it on the china plate which is balanced on the arm of the chair I'm half sitting, half perching in. I move forward to its edge otherwise it will engulf me. Mrs Hannah has a high hard chair. 'If I sat in that low one, I'd never get up.'

She talks and I listen. She tells me how when her son got a place at Dundee University and she asked Miss Lewenz the headmistress of the High School for a day off to take him up there, she was refused.

'You wouldn't be paid,' Miss L said immediately.

'Oh no, I wouldn't expect to be. I just need the day off.'

Miss L considered.

'No,' she said. 'Sorry. It just can't be done. It would set a precedent.'

Mrs Hannah tells me that her colleagues were all incensed.

'They all came to me and they said, Look here Nansi, you go, never mind her, we'll cover for you. So when I'd taught the period before lunch – it was the Upper Fifth I think – I told them. Now I'm not going to be here after lunch, I'm going to Dundee. And you're all going to sit here and be jolly quiet and behave yourselves and not say a word to anyone.'

'And you got away with it?'

Mrs Hannah laughs. 'I did!'

'She never knew?'

'I don't know. I don't think so. Well, not a word was ever said.'

*

Now, this is considered by the grown-ups and teachers and in fact the whole crowd to be fun, this thing of jumping along in an old sack till you reach the end or else fall over. But maybe the parents aren't as interested as they should be? I notice that many of the Mums are just standing squinting into the sun and chatting, arms folded, bags hanging on their shoulders, as if they've quite forgotten they're there to watch their daughters race. One or two have brought dogs on leads. A small black one, perhaps a puppy, rolls over and over on the grass. Another Mum is holding a thermos of tea, smoking a cigarette. It's not my Mum. Mine is over there in the white trousers, huge sunglasses, wedge sandals with cork soles. She's the youngest Mum there and the prettiest. She's talking to Susie L's Mum, who is old and grey-haired and holding a Jessops carrier bag.

Meanwhile the sun beats down and my sack comes up to my chest and I have to pull it up till my arms really hurt because if I don't it will go bunchy and loose and I'll trip and fall over.

'Now girls,' Mrs Rogers says and she screws up her eyes in a way that's meant to be friendly, 'you've all been practising really hard in the heats, you should be good at this by now.'

'On your marks . . .'

*

Mrs Hannah tells me how she came to teach PE.

'Well, after the war there was a dearth of teachers. I enrolled at the London College of Dance – I learned ballroom, Cecchetti method, paso doble and Greek – you know – Natural Movement. And then Betty and Dil Hancock, who were my husband's godmothers, they were running this school, the Wyvil, since about 1920-something and I don't know why but they came to me and said: Oh dear we haven't got anyone to do games!

'Well, I was a dancer by training but I supposed I could teach physical fitness and so I agreed to go and fill in. Nothing was said but after the first term I asked them what was happening and they said, Well, we'd rather hoped you'd stay on. So that was it, you see – that's how I found myself teaching games at the Wyvil School. Oh and they were very funny about paying – there was no salary or anything – they just said, Tell us how many hours you've done my dear, and they gave you some money just like that.'

The sun moves slowly around Mrs Hannah's sitting room till it's so bright in our faces that we have to move. She starts to tell me about the breast cancer she had years ago, the mastectomy – all of this while she was teaching us ('I only had six weeks off after the operation then straight back to school!') – the people she's known who have died. I know why this is, why we talk like this.

It's because we're getting on well and there's unexpected warmth between us and talking of PE has slipped naturally into talking of other things – such as the way we've both dealt with the things which have happened to us in the years since we both stood in the same gymnasium and she told me to stretch my arms out and I stretched them. It was so cold in that gym, and here we are now, two grown-ups in a warm place somewhere in an unknown future and it seems like the right and natural conversation to be having, but it also squeezes my heart, I don't know why.

She asks me whether I exercise now and I confess I don't, not enough, but I do Pilates for my back, have done it for years. She nods approvingly. 'Core stability.'

'That's right,' I say. 'If only I'd done it before I had my babies, it would have made such a difference.'

We both sigh.

'Something strange,' Mrs Hannah says, 'about having you here, seeing you here after all these years. But nice, very nice,' she adds quickly.

She asks about my life and I'm not sure how I end up telling her about my parents' messy divorce, how my father later killed himself.

'You poor poor girl!'

I immediately feel guilty for eliciting sympathy and try to explain to her that it wasn't quite like that – that he'd died for me so many years before. When people are shocked for me I always feel it's a drama I haven't quite earned. The real hurt he caused me was something altogether deeper yet more ordinary and banal too.

Mrs Hannah sighs and tells me about some sisters she knew – 'The youngest was a lovely girl, used to come over and walk our dog, look.'

She picks up some snaps of a golden Labrador, two golden Labradors on the lawn I now recognise out there through the window. 'That one's the mother, that one's the daughter – yes I know, it looks like it should be the other way round.

'Anyway she used to come round all the time. Then one day they drove up to see their father and the car came off the road in rain and turned over and they managed to get her sister – who was driving – out, but, well, she drowned. She was a beautiful young girl, clever and happy and so much promise – a place at university, everything ahead of her.'

Actually I don't know if the fine details of this story as I've written them down are completely correct – because I can't write them down. I know there was a bright and beautiful young girl and I know there was a death in a car, a death by drowning. I know the dogs were involved somehow, somewhere. But – though I am a writer and I know people expect and even want writers to write things down – I don't know why I'm here any more with my old PE teacher who has stopped giving orders and is sitting still for once. All I know is, it no longer feels quite so right to make notes.

*

We wait, tensed up in the starting line. I try not to think of the race, I try not to think of the moment when it will all be over, when everyone will have stopped looking and shouting and caring. The moment of peace and quiet.

In the early mornings I lie in bed and talk to my Panda, his sweet, calm black and white face on my pillow. Panda and I have perfect peace and quiet. Sometimes he thinks things and sometimes he doesn't. Mostly he just keeps quiet and looks at me as I tell him stuff about my day. Daddy said he once read in the News of the World how a little girl left a Panda at an airport and never saw him again. He wasn't where she left him, he wasn't in Lost Property, he wasn't Anywhere. Maybe he got on a plane to China, said Daddy, laughing to himself. He told the story as though it was funny, but every time I let myself think about it, it fills me with dread.

I think the warm, quiet thought of Panda now as I wait and try to watch Mrs Rogers' lips to see the moment when she is about to blow her whistle.

*

I always come first in spelling but I don't mind that. Here is the classroom where I learn to spell 'prince' and 'discover' and 'salutation'. Ye Old Salutation is a pub in the centre of town but it's a greeting too.

'Salutations!' says Charlotte the spider in *Charlotte's Web*.

On the cover of the Puffin paperback, Fern the child has a high-up brown ponytail, the sort I want. I try to stretch my own hair up into a ponytail like Fern's but it won't fit, it's too short, it will always be too short and kinked.

To make long hair, my sisters and I wear tights on our heads. We put the knicker bit on our heads and let the leg bits dangle free. Then we look in the mirror and fling the long pieces back over our shoulders as if it's a bother, as if it's in our way. My big ambition is to have hair that gets in the way, to have a teacher ask me to Please Tie It Back. I would love to be a girl who has to tie her hair back.

The most popular girls at school have to remove all their jewellery for games and wear their hair Tied Back. I remove nothing, I come as I am, unbejewelled, short-haired, in my gym knickers and Aertex shirt.

*

One of the things in the playground is a big concrete piece of tunnel. The Big Pipe, it's called. You can sit inside it and chat, three girls in a row, and eat a Kit-Kat with your buckled navy shoes high on the inner curve so the wafer crumbs fall in the lap of your (pink or blue spotted poplin) summer dress. Or you can climb right up on top of it and let go. Your skirt will ride up as you push off to slide down, and your pants need to be slippy ones or you'll get stuck halfway. You'll land on knee-grazing asphalt, gritty and cracked with small weeds, darkened by recent rain.

I never climb on it and I never slide off. That's for daring girls. Once you join the queue there's no going back. If you didn't slide, someone would push you, and hard. And I don't sit inside and talk either as no one ever saves me a place. The same three girls always get in there every break time. Occasionally a new person may be let in, but it will be for certain unspoken reasons and it won't be just anyone. If you attempt to get in there, all they need to do is give you a quick and vicious look to remind you of your place.

The teachers never see this. The teacher on duty always imagines the children are playing fairly, happily, innocently. She walks around dreaming in her long brown coat, imagining life makes a sweet kind of sense for these children. What she doesn't know is that the rules are complex and brutal and that there are no second chances. Blood will be spilled if they are broken.

On the other side of the playground there's another tunnel – a long low, much smaller one for the babies. The Little Pipe, it's called. I sit on that. You can sit astride it and pretend it's an engine or a horse while the babies get on their hands and knees and crawl through it – Kindergarten, Lower Prep. I do that. When I've eaten my biscuits and had my milk that's what I do, sit astride it and tell myself I'm galloping over the prairies and hope no one will ever ask me to leave that safe, wide, open plain and do anything else I don't want to do.

*

Her father went to this exact same school, the Wyvil, when he was young in the 1930s. He says it was a vicious time, he says he hated it.

'When Miss Hancock was younger,' he says, 'she had a stick. Can you imagine it?'

She tries to – tries to think of Miss Hancock young and slim and quick enough to wield a stick. She's surprised to find she can, quite easily.

She tells him that one of the teachers — Miss Witty — still has a stick now. Well, it's a magic wand, a collapsing one — the sort that Sooty uses — but if she's cross she makes it go stiff and she whacks hands with it.

He looks at her as if she's said something unsurprising. He finishes his cigarette and lights a new one from it.

'That's nothing,' he says, sucking to make the cigarette come alight. 'We were whacked with a cane.'

'Ouch!'

'Yes. Exactly.'

She gazes at him, in this strange competition of pain they're having, and wonders, why does he send her to this school? If they used to hit him there when he was a boy, then why? But she never dares ask him the real questions. He makes her feel responsible for the answers, something she cannot bear. Instead she asks him if he ever did PE?

'Nope. Got out of it. My heart.'

'What?'

'I had a heart condition.'

'What's that?'

'Well actually it was nothing. They got it wrong, didn't they? Ha! Turned out there was nothing wrong with me at all, perfectly healthy I was. But they thought I had, so I got out of it. Never did any exercise at school at all. Sat out on the sidelines and watched. Good, eh?'

*

It's not just Miss Hancock and Miss Betty. Some of the other teachers who taught my Dad are still here, though they're incredibly old. Some are almost dead.

Miss Brunner for instance who takes prayers and wiggles her thumbs when she says the Lord's Prayer. Give us this day our daily bread – wiggle, wiggle. Standing in the very front row, the Kindergarten row, I get a perfect view of the thumbs. The skin is very crinkled, the nails are thick and yellow like a dead person's nails. I shut my eyes, screw them so tightly shut that I see space and stars, and I think about Tom-Tom the Piper's Son. But when I open them again the nails are still there, surrounded by flashing floaty lights. For ever and ever amen.

When all the teachers finally die of old age and the daily bread is all stale and mouldy, then the school will have to close down. Daddy says that day cannot be far off.

*

'On your marks . . .'

The Mums and Dads are all quite still, watching. Someone smiles because they like the idea of races so much. Are they mad?

[66]

'Get set . . .'

There is a little cabbage white butterfly flickering over the crowd, he has no idea that a race is about to happen. Faces lean forward, the sacks are pulled up tight. Cabbage white could not care less. His movements are all jerky, up and down, like he hasn't yet made up his mind where he's going and he has all the time he needs. Mrs Rogers takes a breath, enjoying it.

'Go!'

The Mums and Dads immediately begin to shout. Even though I was ready to go, even though my foot was there all ready to take off, how did I manage to hesitate? Did I watch the butterfly a second too long and not start in time? I'm already too late. Before I've even begun I'm last.

'Come on! Come on!'

*

Here I am at twelve, heading for thirteen. No real breasts yet but if I jump up and down naked in front of the bathroom mirror, something happens, something moves.

My sisters watch from the bath, fascinated. I laugh and jump sideways – a ballet dancer doing pas de chat. Something jiggles. I'm thin so it's obvious. Flesh and fatness under the skin, just coming out of nowhere. I'm changing shape so slowly and secretly that I have to jump like a cat to see it.

I'm almost thirteen and all I want is to be graceful,

beautiful. I have a pair of pale pink satin ballet shoes. I darn the ends like real ballerinas do. The soles are white leather and they smell of wooden floors, music, perfection. Alone in my bedroom, I close the door and sniff the shoes then put them on, tie the ribbons perfectly, criss-cross and tucking in the ends. Standing in front of the mirror in nightie and ballet shoes, I grip the table and raise myself onto my toes even though these are not pointe shoes. My toes curl, tense, then take my weight. I let go for a second and half shut my eyes to imagine how this might look if it were real.

*

'Now this, Upper Four D, is a horse,' says Mrs Rogers, patting the brown suede rump of a thing that looks like anything but.

The horse has four legs, it's true, but they are shiny brown wooden sticks, splayed out at an angle. There are four of these so-called horses in the gym. Four horses, fifteen thick hard ropes hanging from the ceiling, twenty-five black rubber mats, stacked so you can sit on top of them, a trampoline, some long brown forms or benches and three walls of bars, shiny bars which go right up to the ceiling.

In the far corner of the gym is a small black upright piano for when they have Assembly in here which they sometimes do especially if it's a Friday. On top of the piano is some sheet music and two tambourines, I don't know why. But this is a horse and I have always eyed it with dread and suspicion.

But now Mrs Rogers pulls it further out into the middle of the room and then she pulls the trampoline round in front of it. She then grimly pulls out one of the large black rubber mats and slaps it down on the floor on the other side. She folds her arms and stands back and looks at this arrangement for a moment. Everything about it makes my stomach dissolve.

'Vaulting practice,' says Mrs Rogers and she squeaks across the floor in her Dunlop Green Flash shoes.

I'm fourteen. Two weeks ago I got my first period. It wasn't much, but I daren't do gym now without a towel between my legs – a fat pad like a thick-sliced piece of white bread, looped onto a horrid belt thing which only just tucks into my gym knickers. Mum says I don't need to wear a pad all the time, but I want to, just for gym anyway. In case it comes back, suddenly.

'It won't be sudden,' Mum says soothingly. 'You'll know.'

'How?'

'You'll feel it. It'll be gradual, like the last time.'

I believe her, but all the same the feel of the pad

is reassuring – what could be worse than to gush suddenly, spurting blood all over the gym floor? I worry, though, that from the back I look like I'm wearing a nappy. So I develop a habit that will last all my school career – of running my hand quickly over my bottom to check its guilty bulk.

Mrs Rogers eyes the horse as if it might bolt.

'Now, Upper Four D, I'm going to have you running, jumping on the trampoline, both hands on the horse and swing your legs up and over – up and over! – like this.'

She doesn't demonstrate herself. Instead she gets Ann W to do it – Ann W who has long muscly legs and short black hair and can do everything sporty and is so fearless she can even shin right up the ropes and look down on the whole gym from the ceiling.

*

The Wyvil School is on Private Road, in Mapperley Park. To get to it, Daddy and I walk up a long, steep, silent road with no other houses on it, just silence and birds tweeting and flies buzzing and scrappy grass. A private road. Groundsel and nettles grow in the verges. A friend of someone we know once saw an adder here or was it a viper?

'Both are poisonous,' my father says, 'but don't worry it wouldn't bite, not unless attacked.' For a brief second I picture my father attacking the snake with his umbrella and the snake baring its teeth and fighting back.

Once we found a feather from a jay bird, a tiny feather, blue and black stripes and small as a flower. My father always smokes a cigarette as we walk and talk about the creatures who may be lurking in the grass. I like hearing about the creatures, even the snakes are all right in the morning. It makes school seem safer and further away, both at the same time. It makes it seem like a place that is floating in the middle of nowhere, like a place in a book.

*

I jump and jump, thudding and thudding along on the grass. The sack smells of hotness — rough, hairy hotness that catches on your hangnails. I think of rats, I can't help it. I can't help knowing that rats may have chewed this sack, just as I chew my own fingernails. I think of this and even though it's hot, my arm hairs stand up and I shiver and wish I was ill in bed with tummy-ache and my Panda. Anything and anywhere but here, but this.

*

At the top of the road, sunk into a crumbling old brick wall, is a window which is the kitchen of the school. The window is dirty — murky and green like algae, never cleaned.

'Oh look,' my father always says in exactly the same voice as we reach the top, 'there's Mr Fishwick!'

Two pale faces relieve the gloom at the window – one is the cook and the other is Mr Fishwick who has a real glass eye. He can take it out and show you if you like. There it lies, slightly sticky in the palm of his hand. I have never seen him do this, but other children have.

Without the eye, the socket would just look like a white hole, my father says, a crater in the skin, though it would be healed up.

'Would there be blood?'

'Yes. Pools of it. Everywhere.'

'Oh!'

'Only joking. No blood. I told you – it's healed.'

I don't want to look, I really don't, but I can't take my eyes off Mr Fishwick. Once you know the hole is there underneath, it's impossible to tug your eyes away, however rude you feel.

Mr Fishwick is a perfectly frank man, Miss Betty says one day, quite out of the blue, as if this were a fact worth noting.

*

We must take it in turns, one after another, to run forward and vault over the horse. There is no choice in the matter, no refusing. My heart thumps harder and harder as my turn approaches. Some girls do it easily. Some girls do not look at all worried or afraid. They just stand there with blank faces as if they're always being made to jump over things.

One after another, they run and jump and vault.

As each girl lands – bare feet first, knees bent – on the mat the other side, Mrs Rogers catches them around the waist and holds them for a second – 'Very good, well done!' – to regain their balance. Then she blows her whistle for the next girl to start. It's true that one or two girls only get over the horse with a little difficulty, and Pamela D nearly winds herself, but most girls get themselves over it one way or another.

'Very nice,' Mrs Rogers says. 'Don't forget to bend your knees – that's right, up, up and over!'

There are only two girls in front of me, Elizabeth A and June S. Then June goes and there is only Elizabeth. Then Elizabeth goes and the room is under-water, slow motion – this is me and the room is a place seen from above, I'm not here, my beating heart has lifted me out of the room, made it possible for me to move forward without really being me.

The whistle blows.

My body and I move quickly towards the trampoline and put my hands on the horse but I know from the start that there's no way I'm going over it.

It's high, I'm small, my legs will not go higher than my head! Instead I do a small pretend jump, more of a bounce, then scramble quickly over the horse on my knees and drop down on the other side. A few girls snigger, but Mrs Rogers ignores them. She holds me gently but firmly round the waist.

'It's all right Julie, never mind, let's try again.'

I blush hard, I can feel the heat in my whole face, but I go back along the huge big room, still under-water, still slowed and dead and breathless. And I do exactly the same thing all over again. This time, Mrs Rogers holds me round the waist as if I've landed on the mat like the other girls. Except we both know I haven't.

She blows her whistle, glances at me quickly with the eye of a bird, eye of an owl.

'All right,' she says. 'Next!'

The running, bouncing and vaulting continues.

There are two other girls who don't get over the horse either. One is fat and one is very small, the youngest girl in the year. Each time, Mrs Rogers does the same thing. Gives another chance and then moves on.

And that is that, it's over. I don't remember that we ever did vaulting again. And maybe the other two will go on to do Bar exams, direct movies, fall in love, be chemists, have babies, work for charity, or write books like me. But one thing is certain: all three of us will progress through our school careers – our whole lives – without ever knowing how it feels to vault a horse.

*

Now Mr Fishwick solemnly waves his hand at you, at the little girl with the satchel and the gingham bow and the stomach full of rose-hip syrup and cod liver oil and fear.

You wave back but your heart sinks and sinks because you hate school, you're so unreasonably afraid of it – afraid of the sharp lessons, the sharp teachers, the sharpness of the other children who always know where to go, of the cold dusty darkness where you can never find your peg, where you need to spend a penny so badly that a bit of wet starts to come, where someone will smack you with a sharp, sharp ruler if you get in the wrong line-up line.

Once, in prayers, a child was just standing singing and suddenly there was a puddle of wet on the parquet floor. Children either side of her were splashed and the mop was fetched by someone with a grim face and the child was led out in front of everyone. She had to wear her gym kit all day. All day everyone knew she was the one who had wet herself because she had her gym kit on, the only child in the school in gym kit all day. You'd have known anyway though. She cried and cried and the skin of her face turned so red, the dark splotchy red of shame. The hotness and wetness of shame.

You were speechless, appalled, afraid. You never want to be that girl.

To make you brave, your Mum puts a dab of her perfume on your hanky so you can breathe in the home and bathroom smell of her. She also sews a little red dog on your gym bag – so you can find it quickly, so you can know it's yours straightaway without having to stand and fill up with panic as you try to spell out your name.

J u l i e   S u s a n   P i k e.

*

Another thing in the playground is a smooth, strong iron bar, worn and shiny and with a rusty redness that comes off on your hands on slightly wet days. If it rains during break then that's Wet Play and we must go in the Hall. But if it rains during lessons and stops for break then we are let out into the damp playground. In summer it smells good when it's damp – of earth and leaves and wetness and sometimes of Wagon Wheel wrappers dropped in the puddles.

The bar has to be dried with a towel fetched from the Lower Prep kitchen. At playtime, some girls get their knees over it and hang upside down, summer dresses falling over their heads. Some do that and then use one hand to bunch them up so you can't see their pants. Rows of white pants and white lacy socks hanging in upside-down rows.

I have brown socks, not white, that's because I'm not popular. At home we eat brown bread, too, and I'm not allowed Clackers ('Too dangerous,' says my Mum, 'a girl broke her wrist!') even though they are the playground craze. I never hang on the bars, I wouldn't dare.

What one girl does is this: she loops just one knee over the bar and holds on with both hands, then she somehow makes herself go over and over, round and round. Everyone watches her and claps. That's all she does, every playtime, just loops herself on and goes round and round to the sound of clapping.

*

Then a strange thing starts to happen. Suddenly, having been almost last, she isn't any more. How is it possible? How can she have moved so fast? She's not a fast girl but a slow girl, a scared and cautious girl, yet suddenly here she is, swooping ahead like another person altogether.

She sees Alison R's shock as she jumps on past her.

She senses girls behind her and she sees a quick flash of her Mum's face: real surprise. And in front of her there's only one girl and it's Sally F who is fastest at everything and now she's even jumped past her.

How could this happen?

She glances down at where she's holding the sack taut over her feet and she can see that each jump covers a great distance, she's jumping jumping in grand, unnatural strides. It's like a dream where she wins. Now the finishing line — held by Miss M and Mrs W — is in sight and she can't believe it, but she just might reach it second or maybe first.

She glances back and sees Jane not far behind. Not far, but far enough. Her normally pale face is dark pink with trying and she looks defeated, stricken, as if she knows she'll never catch up.

*

When she was about four years old, her sisters even younger, they told her Daddy that he was going to die. He was only in his thirties but they told him he had just a few months left to live. Something wrong with his liver. He was a grown-up but he panicked. He lay down on the carpet and pressed his hand to his side and he said he could feel it — his large, diseased liver — and he screamed and cried without taking breath just like a baby.

She does not remember this as she was too much of a baby herself. But she remembers the carpet —

blue with a rose pattern and the kind of fluff that comes off on your clothes. She thinks it might have been shocking, to see a man, a whole big Daddy, on a carpet.

He lay down on this carpet and he screamed and cried.

*

She hates scrambled egg, especially the black burnt bit, and she tells lies whenever she can, to get away with things. She has no choice – there are so many things she must avoid such as school, deep water, sharks and clothes which have to go on over her head. She is afraid of hairwashes and afraid of catching balls, of things catching fire, of PE, of germs and of talking to people she doesn't know. She is afraid she'll get picked to read in class or that someone will want to play with her. She is afraid, too, that this won't happen.

At break time she stands in a corner of the playground and pretends to be incredibly interested in the wall, holding her breath and staring at the deep cracks and fissures of it, hoping and hoping no one will speak to her. Actually, she is quite genuinely interested in the wall. She watches the beetles coming and going, clambering in and out of the Bunter Sandstone. Bunter Sandstone – that's what it is – it's what Nottingham's made of. It's so crumbly that the beetles end up with a dusting of creamy yellow all over their neat shiny backs.

She is seven and she reads the *Famous Five* books and now there is a man in the garden watching her, she is sure there is. He might be anyone – he might be a gypsy or a crook or a man with a revolver hidden about his person.

'Look!' she tells her sisters. 'Don't look now but there's a man out there. We should do something.'

Her sisters look.

'I said don't look!'

They tell her there's no one. She looks again herself. There's no one, just a lawn and a tree and some wind.

'What are you three doing?' asks their Daddy (who after several years is still alive after all, because the doctors got it wrong, his liver was just an especially good-sized and healthy liver – hooray!).

She glances at the end of the lawn. The man steps back into the bushes, revolver in his hand. Her sisters look at her and look back at the lawn and she wonders if they see him too.

'Nothing!' they all shout and run inside.

*

The thing is, if I slow down just for the smallest moment, Jane can catch me up. Even just the act of having this thought makes me go a little slower, makes my whole heart slow down. There are races and then there is friendship. Friendship, surely, is about not racing, but waiting: keeping up, catching up? Jane is my very best friend — actually my first ever best friend. How, I wonder, would it feel to beat her, my only friend? Terrible is the answer. Shaming. Unthinkable.

I don't stop, of course I don't. But I just don't push my chest out quite so far, I let a little of the fizz come out of me, which means I don't hop along so hard and fast. It would be best of course if we both won together, if I came first and she came second, or maybe the other way round, it doesn't matter much, everyone knows there's not much difference beween 1 and 2.

If I was the sort who wins things, I might be allowed to grow my hair like Jane's, get a ponytail. In my head I see us both, hair tied back with bright red ribbons — Play-Doh friends!

*

In the summer term we do our absolute best to get to school really early because if we get there early enough, i.e. before ten to nine, then we're allowed to knock up before Assembly.

I do it with Jackie and Jackie and Jacqui. The three Jackies and me. Some of us take our hymn books out onto the tennis courts with us so we're completely ready and then all we have to do is fling our rackets back through the open window of our form room and we can go straight into Assembly from playing tennis. The tennis courts are right outside our classroom which is A5 this year, the Lower Fifth year. Some girls jump out of the bay window and down the rockery but if you're caught doing that you're in big trouble. It makes sense to go round. But then you need to try and get a court.

Arthur Ashe beat Connors at Wimbledon last year.

My tennis racket is a Spalding. Jackie says that's a stupid racket to have, a wet racket. She and Jacqui have Dunlops. The other Jackie has a Slazenger. The Jackies are my friends but it's true we don't have much in common. My parents are divorced, theirs are all still together. I have brown bread in my packed lunch, they have white. On Saturday mornings I still have ballet classes and stand pointing and stretching in white tights and pink satin, while they go into town and buy make-up and look for boys and some-times they find them.

*

The Senior gym changing rooms are quite different from the Lower School ones, which are tiny and just off the Covered Way.

The Senior ones are under A5 and A4, quite close to the headmistress's office. You go down some steps into what was once cellars and a sign says Mind Your Head, Do Not Jump so everyone of course jumps the last three steps. Down here, it smells of rubber and feet. There are banks and banks of lockers. The light is just a bulb hanging like a prison light. Down here a man was once found with his throat cut. Suicide.

'Oh yeah?'

'Yeah, seriously. My Mum said. It was in the papers. The man who built this house – Clarence Lodge.'

'When?'

'Don't know. Eighteen seventy-something.'

'Before it was a school?'

'Of course before it was a school, you dingbat. These were the cellars. You think he'd kill himself in the gym changing room?'

*

Life gets darker and darker. The Miners' Strike, the coal shortage. There's no heating on in school so there are three advantages: we can wear our own clothes just like the sixth-formers. We can go home early (it's too cold by two thirty). And no games! It's far too cold to get undressed for anything.

At home there are power cuts and we come to love them too. All the lights go out and we heat baked beans on a little stove that you light with a match and lots of candles. Apart from having no TV, you could say it's a near perfect existence.

*

In the darkest part of winter, in the flat, dead middle of the week (Wednesday afternoons) they get a bus to hockey. It's a green double-decker hired just for them and it moves sadistically up Arboretum Street at ten to two and waits outside the black iron gates like a beast waiting for its prey. They are counted on at school and off at the other end, but the teachers don't come on the bus. They drive to the field separately, in Mrs Rogers' warm and comfy car.

'So they can smoke,' says Diane M.

All the teachers smell of smoke all the time and especially after break. Every time the staffroom door swings open and shut, smoke billows out. If you didn't know that they all smoked then you would think the room was on fire.

The playing fields are seven miles away at Redhill. The bus stops on the main road and you walk up past neat bungalows with mown lawns and crazy paving, to where the smooth road with its neat verge peters into a rough track. Poppies and dandelions and dog shit. Up this track is a modern block of changing rooms with showers, beyond them empty flat purplish fields, spiritless and bleak, the occasional woman in a warm sheepskin walking a Labrador along the same muddy track they use for cross-country.

Hard to believe that these are the same fields where they have Sports Day – green and warm and covered in white clothes and flags and parents. The summer feels like another country. In winter up here, their thighs turn purple, their veins ache, their breath freezes. It's said that once a girl died of cold up here.

'It's not true.'

'No, of course it isn't.'

Deaths of girls are great diversions, always listened to with equal amounts of fear and fascination. They all remember the girl who was electrocuted by a hairdryer in the bath – the head announcing it to a hushed Assembly the next morning. It seemed un-believable that she'd been sitting at a desk in A Block just the day before and now she was dead. Then there was the girl whose hair caught fire in full view of everyone at the Carol Service – but she survived and anyway her hair was way too long and frizzy, she shouldn't have been sitting in front of a candle.

Actually the place you are most likely to die is the bus to hockey. The driver doesn't want to know, and all the teachers care about is counting them off at the other end, so the bus is a place of torture. The whole of the morning is overshadowed by the cloud of getting on that bus. Loud girls with names like Vicky and Alison hitting you on purpose with their bags, smoking upstairs and committing vandalism.

Writing words like Cunt and Intercourse on the maroon seat backs in marker pen.

It's not enough, though, for these girls to be bad. They want all the good girls to be bad too. They want to get the whole world on the top deck and make them do things they'll regret, to give them power over you later. Some girls give in. Some girls who would never normally dream of smoking cigarettes give in and do it on the bus to hockey.

*

Summer's here. In the playground, wallflowers are out. Their thick sweetness drifts into the classrooms and you can hear the crowds of bees even when you are in French. The classrooms get hot and tired — smell of old tennis balls and yoghurt-smeared spoons, sliced bread and Marmite squashed in a polythene bag, sweaty sandals, white socks stained black at the toe.

Someone's French penfriend is in the playground — Merielle or Isabelle — an exotic bird with a long ponytail and in her own clothes. Everyone pretends not to look at her. The girl whose penfriend she is becomes instantly more popular — for a week or so. Girls knock up on the tennis courts, but not the big girls — the big girls are doing exams. The doors are covered in white paper so you can't look in. Teachers have even harder faces when they become invigilators. But it's summer and suddenly they all have on sleeveless dresses – always the same dresses as last year – their upper arms mottled and tired and begging to be covered.

You glimpse the wisps of underarm hair as they explain a maths question. Sometimes, as they bend over you, you smell it too – an unwashed smell so strong it gets into your mouth.

*

When you, my first baby, turn out to be a boy, I'm secretly astonished. I'm a woman with sisters, aunts, grandmothers. Apart from one mad grandfather who barely counts, I grew up surrounded by femaleness. Even our dog was a girl. How could something so male have come out of my soft, worried, uncompeting female body?

It's a boy. You're a boy. She has a boy. I am the mother of a boy. I have to practise the words in private, to get used to them. And when the midwives come round to weigh and check and laugh and make notes, they talk as though a boy were quite a normal thing to have, and I hear myself joining in with such conviction.

Later, though, in the warm silence after my bath, our bath, I study my naked boy intently and I still can't take you in. For a while, though you have a name, I simply call you My Boy. Our boy. Where's our boy? I ask J when I want to feed you. Or: Is that our boy I can hear crying? And though I would never admit it to anyone because of how it sounds, deep inside I know my boy will be strong and fast, that you will win races and play games and be a hero. Because you're a boy. I don't know much about boys but I know this. Boys are good at games, boys try, boys win.

But –

But one day you will be bigger than me and then what? I won't think about that now. When I put you to sleep in the middle of the bed – a tiny knitted sausage in his white cellular blanket – and I see you in my mind's eye in the future putting on a helmet and climbing onto a motorbike, I burst into tears.

*

'Oh yes, I remember you,' says Mrs Rogers when I track her down with help from Nancy, the current headteacher's assistant, and ring her number in Nottingham.

'Oh goodness, surely not?'

It's not like Mrs Hannah. I had Mrs Hannah at two separate schools and she taught us for dance as well as PE and I was quite good at dance – well, in my way. But I'm completely unable to believe I made any sort of impression at all on Mrs Rogers, who was pure games – a teacher who lived in a track-suit and did not understand those who could not keep up. Hockey, netball, rounders, tennis, cross-country runs. Ninety-odd girls in each year, a thousand girls in the school, most of them able to score and win and even vault horses but not me, absolutely not me.

There's a little click on the phone as Mrs Rogers takes a breath.

'Oh yes,' she says, 'I remember your hairstyle.'

My hairstyle. My hair in those days was as it would be now if it weren't for a little chemical interven-tion: mousy brown and neither curly nor straight, the plainest of plain hair – except with vicious little kinks in it.

'Gas-oven hair,' my Mum jokingly called it when I was a teenager.

'Why?'

'Because it makes you want to put your head in a gas oven.'

I realise that while talking to Mrs Rogers on the phone I am picturing her wearing a tracksuit. But she's got to be over eighty. She doesn't sound it. She sounds as though she's about to tell us all to get in the showers. She says she's about to go away to stay with friends for a few days and then a week or so after that she's off on a cruise.

'Gosh, you're busy!'

'Well,' she gives a little laugh, 'my knees aren't so good but I manage.'

She says I can come and visit her in between if I like.

*

Right from the start you behave – well, if not like a boy, then like someone else – someone who didn't come out of me. You don't move carefully around the world as I did, as I do, but rather you use the world to launch and propel yourself, fearlessly and perfectly, as if adventure were your right.

The first time you throw yourself backward off the sofa into my arms, I'm just not ready.

'Darling – you can't just do that!'

I catch you but I'm shocked, you might have broken your arm, your leg, your neck. You can only laugh at my surprise and fear and I sigh with relief as I feel your whole body relax against mine. You're wearing red cord dungarees with tartan round the edges. You're two and I'm thirty and we're both in heaven. By the time you're four years old, we've visited St Thomas' A&E no less than three times.

*

I catch a bus to Mrs Rogers' house from Nottingham city centre. Or at least, I'm thinking of getting a taxi and about to ask in Dolcis shoe shop where the rank is, when I see a bus that actually says Carlton on it. Just up near where Griffin and Spalding used to be.

'Do you go up Brecknock Road?'

The bus driver gives me a helpful and friendly look. 'Depends which end. It's a long road.'

'Oh dear. I'm not sure.'

'Where are you going?'

I tell him Mrs Rogers' address.

'Yep! We go there. Jump on ducks. I'll tell you when we get there.'

I get on and sit near the driver. The bus is rather new and clean, the seats scritchy. In front of me a man with dirty jeans and a black beard is talking to himself.

*

The bus drops me at the right end of the road. The driver pulls up just short of the roadworks which are close to the bus stop. 'Straight over the road, left at the lights.'

The roadworks force me off the pavement and I have to follow the arrow and make my way round the edge of a deep asphalt hole surrounded by cones.

An empty Nurishment can rolls around in the gutter.

I cross at the pelican crossing and enter the loop of road where Mrs Rogers now lives. It's a warm day, sun blowing in and out of the clouds, washing on lines, dogs on leads. A man goes past with a Staffordshire bull terrier and asks if I'm lost. I say I'm not, thanks. There are a lot of houses here. Mrs Rogers is at number thirty-something but I can see it goes into the hundreds. Each neat bungalow has a square of clipped garden in front. There's soap suds in the gutter from a recent car wash. A cat stretches out on the bonnet of another (dry) car. Silence except for the faraway crackle of a TV or radio, wind chimes sounding in a clean porch.

*

Now all previous fear has dissolved. Not fear of water – that remains – but fear of remaining afloat, of surviving and breathing and living another day despite that dark cold space, that's gone. She's a proper swimmer, her Dad says as they drive home from the baths, her long hair soaking her anorak.

These days she really enjoys the shock of diving in, the extreme difference it makes to your existence when your whole body suddenly goes wet.

In fact, though she's not much good at crawl –

where your whole face and head has to stay under the water – she's pretty fast at breaststroke, so fast in fact that Mrs Rogers picks her for the Swimming Gala.

'But darling that's great,' says her Mum as she rinses out the breakfast bowls and loads the dishwasher. 'I never even dreamed you'd be picked!'

Neither did she. She's never picked for anything. She couldn't believe it when Mrs Rogers read out her name from the pad without even looking up. Only she felt the private swoop of surprise in her heart, the rush of anxiety at the idea of competing.

But she wants to do it, she does. She prays she won't get her period that day. She doesn't.

On the actual day she's nervous but she swoops into the water and easily comes second. Easily because the fact is she doesn't actually try that hard, she doesn't have to. The water just moves on past her body and she feels the startling rush of going faster than she even thought possible. Her body feels smooth, mechanical almost, like a machine she has finally learned to use. And the lanes, divided up with bright plastic floats, make it easier not harder as she'd feared – you don't have to worry about being bumped by someone. The rush of the pool echoes in her ears and she's second.

Second!

'Well done,' Mrs Rogers tells her for what is probably the first time ever. 'Very good, well tried, well done.'

She thinks Mrs Rogers is going to know it was too easy, that she should have tried harder, that she ought to come first next time. But she doesn't. This time it seems that second is enough. She's done it, she's made the teacher happy – or, if not happy exactly, then satisfied.

She smiles. The water falls from her body as she pushes up from the side, her knee grazing gently on the edge of the pool. She stands up and people are looking at her in her blue school swimsuit. She can feel all the long lean muscles of her body holding her up. She thinks of the thread down your middle, like in ballet. She feels almost graceful, almost strong.

She came second.

It wasn't that hard – maybe she could actually have come first if she'd tried just that tiny bit harder. Ann W came first and is standing there shaking with the effort. But not her, she's not shaking at all. She takes a happy, calm breath and for the first time in her life she genuinely wonders what it might be like to win.

*

Your first Sports Day in the Nursery at Macaulay
C. of E. Primary School. My boy. You're three and a
half exactly – fair-haired, blue-eyed, similar in build
to the way I was at your age, but without my light-
ness and my awkwardness. There's a stability to my
boy, as if your feet are firmly rooted on the ground.
Whereas I was always anxious and wavering, ready
to float off like a balloon.

Mrs S walks around putting plastic markers down
on the playground. Blonde bobbed hair, navy
cropped trousers, thin cardigan, serious face. But
she's not like Mrs Hannah used to be. She's parent-
friendly, child-friendly, she's 'Liz' to us. She's a firm
enough teacher and runs the Nursery with a notice-
able passion, but there are no theatricals, no Them
and Us. She has a whistle but you can tell she's not
used to it and uses it tentatively, only when she has
to. When she moves along the lines, grown-ups don't
scatter out of her way. Instead they get their cameras
ready, or make a joke, or ask if they can be of any
help.

*

You watch with an expression I can only call interest.
You don't really know what's happening or why
you're here but that's all right – you're happy, totally
happy, trusting. So far in your small life, things have

always turned out safe, turned out fun. You know
nothing of dread or worry or responsibility. I don't
even think you know about death – no pets have
died and neither have any grandparents. Once,
outside Peter Jones, you spotted a pigeon and asked
me whether it was dead or alive?

'What pigeon?' I said, struggling to put carrier
bags, babies and pushchair in the car.

'The one out there. Was it dead or not?'

'I really don't know darling. I didn't see it I'm
afraid.'

'The one with its legs in the air!'

Now you sit on a rug under the tree on the grassy
part of the playground and drink squash from a
beaker and wave at me, beaming.

You'll run races, wear a sunhat, drink a drink, run
a relay, balance a wooden cube on a spoon – you'll
do whatever they want you to do. You'll even get in
a sack and jump if that's what's required. Well, why
not? You don't mind whether you come first or last,
not especially.

People like you don't need ribbons. Sports Day
was made for people like you. You have friends –
girls and boys, animals, everyone. Children like you,
grown-ups like you, everyone likes you. One time
we were coming back from shopping and you saw
a lady in the street with hair a bit like Grandma's

and you just opened your arms and ran towards her and she laughed and I had to explain to her that she looked a bit like my Mum, but inside my heart was thumping at the amount of trust you had for everyone. Where did it come from? What was it for? What would happen to it as you grew older?

*

At school they don't have a pool of their own so they have to swim in the Boys' High School Pool. The boys' school has everything theirs doesn't have: a swimming pool, bigger grounds called a Quad, a proper theatre for plays, language labs, boys. This is because the boys' school is old and grand, whereas the girls' school is only a hundred years old and girls haven't been allowed to be clever and have jobs for long.

The girls don't like using the boys' langage labs as all the earphones are greasy and waxy from boys using them. But they have to, otherwise they won't have an Equal Opportunity to do well in French and German, their teacher says. The pool, too. The girls have to be allowed to swim. It's just that you don't like to think about what or who has been in it.

Audrey R says you can get pregnant by swimming in the pool after the boys have been in.

'No you can't,' says Laura F.

'You can. If they've wanked in it you can.'

'Boys can't wank while they swim.'

'Yes they can. How would you know anyway?'

Laughter.

'Of course they can. They can do anything with their hands if they're just standing in the shallow end and doing nothing. Under the water so the teacher can't see.'

'But – the seeds can't live in water.'

'They can, of course they can, they're born to survive, otherwise how do they swim up to the woman's thingy?'

I think of the tadpole drawings in biology. My Mum has told me plenty about sex, more even than I asked for. But I don't know much about what boys can do in water.

'But,' says Laura, 'the chlorine must kill them?'

Audrey shrugs.

'Or if it half kills them, what then?'

'What?'

'Well, you get a spastic baby don't you?'

More laughter.

*

To get to the pool, you have to allow at least ten minutes. You have to go across a grand paved court-yard with shadows on the walls, between lawns and flower beds and into the school with its strange dark boy smells. Everywhere are loud noises and rucksacks with biro writing all over them. The labels on the pegs are all written on and torn. The corridors are more scuffed than in the girls' school, probably because boys go in dirtier places.

The swimming pool changing rooms are dark, damp and echoey. Lucky girls have letters about periods and verrucas. Embarrassing but the brief moment of shame is worth it to get off swimming. Girls stare longingly at the Safe Ones as they sit out the lesson warm and dry. Shoes and socks and blouses and underwear still firmly on. They hold their French vocab books in their hands but everyone knows they're chatting about boys. Everyone else stands and shivers in a miserable way, feet cold on the wet tiles, as they wait for Mrs Rogers to blow on her whistle.

'Lower Five D! Pu-lease!'

Then you dive in. You're given no time to wait. If you don't dive you'll be pushed from behind. You dive in.

The pool is long and in a dark room – not natural light, no sunshine. You dive into the water and for a while you're in a black and silent space – ears stopped, eyes closed, hair drifting.

Is death like this?

Then you burst back up into the shrieking and

the echo of water falling and the blowing of the whistle.

Mrs Rogers' feet are level with your eyes on the poolside, dry and warm: clean white trainers, properly laced, clean white socks, rolled at the top. The world is divided into the wet and the dry, the dead and the living.

'If anyone ever got pregnant by swimming in a pool,' Sarah L later points out, 'it would be on the news all the time and we'd hear about it, wouldn't we?'

*

She can run if she needs to, if it suits her, if she has to.

She remembers a day when she has to run for a good reason. A morning in the summer of seventy-one when her parents are out at work and her sisters playing upstairs and her Granny is standing there in the kitchen ironing and there are tears coming out of her eyes silently and dropping on the ironing-board cover.

'Granny?' she says, a hot rush in her chest. 'What is it? Why are you crying?'

Granny looks at her and pulls out her handkerchief, cries loud and uncontrollably.

'Your parents – they're going to divorce and I'm so sad about it, so sad, oh my love –'

'What?' She stares at her Granny, trying to listen to the black and spiky words she just said.

And the Granny looks back at her granddaughter and realises how irresponsible she's just been and her face fills up with shame and horror, but before she can say anything the girl has turned and run from the room.

And she tries so hard to call the little girl back but the girl is gone – so swiftly out of that open back door, over the patio, over the lawn, stopping only a second by the barns to kick off the raffia sandals that make it hard to run and then she's off, tearing up over the fields, long brown legs getting her along the rough path, up towards the top field where the land stops belonging to her father and becomes another place – the woods, the farm, the rest of the world.

And she can hear the grandmother calling out to her from down the bottom field, desperately crying and calling out – 'Julie! Julie!' – saying over and over that she is sorry, that she doesn't know why she said that awful thing and that she just wasn't thinking and it's not true and now she feels so very terrible.

But the girl ignores her. In fact the very act of ignoring buffs and smarts the wound, gives her some pleasure, though the sobbing in her own head is louder than ever. But she makes herself deaf to everything but the thud of breath in her throat that comes from having run so fast and the bang of the heart-beat that makes her feet keep on running till she finds a soft, hidden grassy place where she can sink down and sob alone and without being found. She flings herself to the ground and she wails and sobs. Far enough away not to be found till she lets herself, till she wants to be.

When the grandmother eventually comes panting up the path and finds her, she holds her tight in her arms, rocking her hard so the girl can smell cough sweets and ironing.

'It's not true,' she says. 'Please say you believe me. I was only being silly my love, it's not true, not true.'

The girl says she believes her. She says so. She cries into her Granny's soft sad body and she says yes she believes her.

Nine months later, her parents are separated, a year later divorced.

And years later, all these years later, it's not really the unhappy sobbing she remembers most clearly and carefully but the joyous cruelty of that lap of honour, the euphoria of that run – oh that long, fast run and the satisfaction of her, the poor grand-mother, left behind, with her shock of words and her angry stream of tears – the joy of her not being able to catch up.

It was spectacular, that run, almost worth all the pain. Brown feet moving over the earth's surface and getting a person from a place she didn't want to be to another she maybe didn't want to be either but at least this was one race that she won. At least there was a choice and she made it. She got herself there to the finish and so very, very uncharacteristically fast.

*

Your first Big School Sports Day. A freezing July day on Clapham Common. Wind bending the trees, parents in fleeces and coats shivering and wishing for cappuccinos.

You're five and a half now, blond hair darkening, your body skinnier than it was at three. You've lost your toddler sturdiness and you look like a thing that might break in the wind. My boy. You sit on a rug with all the other children, picking at a scab on your knees. You look so far away. I love you so hard it hurts my head, my face. I have your small sister and brother in a navy blue tartan double buggy.

You're straining to look for me – unworried, unhurried – and you spot me and give me a small shy smile, then you mouth a grown-up hello. Not too friendly in case someone sees. When the time comes for your race you go and stand in place. Your legs are thin and bendy. You tremble there on the edge of the line, front foot edging forward, ready and eager to go.

You come first in egg and spoon and second in running. I am so proud, so bursting with it. I stand and cheer loudly from the side, willing myself not to cry so people can see. In the end I cheer so hard and loud that your baby brother starts crying instead and I'm glad to have a chance to pick him up and press my nose and mouth into the hot flannel warmth of his Babygro.

*

But my slowing-down has a huge, untold effect, the whole scene ripples and changes. Now suddenly there are girls all in front of me, passing me and most of all Jane — Jane is jumping and jumping on ahead, past me, past everyone — jump, jump, jump — and she's looking happy and then everyone's cheering especially Bobby her Mum and the next thing we know it's all over and Jane's climbing herself out of her sack and getting — a red ribbon.

Mrs Rogers is pinning it on her shirt and Jane is grinning in happiness and pride. I go past her and hand in my sack, drop it on the piles with the other sacks, used and deflated. Jane looks at me and licks her lips. Inside my heart is tumbling down to a place it's never been.

'I waited for you,' I croak, tears creeping into my voice. 'Didn't you see? I waited for you.'

She laughs as if she hasn't heard.

'Well —' she gives me a pitying look and blinks a bit.

'Well what?'

'Well that was silly, wasn't it?'

Her Mum — grey hair, navy cardigan — hugs and kisses her. My Mum — white flared trousers, sunglasses propped on her head — asks what on earth possessed me to slow down?

*

'Well, you weren't a games person, were you?' says Mrs Rogers from her armchair on the other side of the room.

She looks just the same except I realise I've probably never seen her sitting down before. I've certainly never seen her without a tracksuit. She rubs her knee. She says she has a new knee. When I told her that she couldn't possibly be expected to remember me unless it was because I was so unsporty, a small part of me secretly hoped she'd disagree. Say I was at least lively. Or a good sport, a good loser. Or hint that I had promise in tennis but lacked confidence. But no. Not a games person. Simple as that. Not now. Not ever.

I laugh — a friendly little laugh.

'No,' I say, 'that's true. I wasn't. I don't know why really.'

'Well, some people are and some aren't and you weren't. Do you do any sport now?'

I wince. 'Pilates?'

She smiles as if that says it all.

We both pause and listen to the faraway sound of an ice-cream van. She sits in silence. She doesn't seem to feel the need to say anything else, to supply the conversation. And after all, I think to myself, why should she? I think of everything she's done for me: showing me how to hold my wrist for a backhand, forcing me to run through the mud at Bestwood in November (and then stand naked in the showers afterwards), giving me at least two chances to throw my body over a horse.

'You told me not to run away from the ball,' I remind her. 'In netball.'

She smiles as if she remembers, but then again she probably says that to all the girls: 'Don't run away from the ball!'

'Yes,' she says, 'that sounds like me.'

She glances down at her feet in their brown lace-ups (not trainers) and suddenly I understand something I never understood before: my old PE teacher is shy.

I notice the long row of china dogs ranged along the top of her gas fire, some arranged in groups, some individually. She sees me looking.

'Westies,' she says. 'I had another Westie – after Jenny, you know.'

'I remember Jenny!' I say, surprised as memories of a small white dog with a slightly stained moustache skitter into view. Jenny making her way on a long red lead along the Covered Way outside Mrs Rogers' office. Mrs Rogers is holding the dog in one arm and locking her office with the other, on her way out to supervise netball practice.

'You don't have one any more?'

'Oh I don't want one now. I don't want some poor dog to outlive me, do I?'

I tell her I understand that.

'Dogs are fun,' I say, thinking of our maniac of a Border collie, 'but a lot of trouble too.'

She nods agreement and pleats her fingers.

'A responsibility. They tie you down.'

'And you're travelling such a lot, with your cruises.'

She looks pleased.

'I am, oh yes, I am.'

*

'I'll tell you something,' says Mrs Rogers. 'Do you remember when we were always having bomb scares?'

'Of course I do. We all loved it because it meant we missed lessons.'

'Well, we'd have to evacuate the whole school out

into the Arboretum and line you all up there and one time the police gave the all-clear and Miss Lewenz turned and said to me, Oh goodness, I don't know how I'm going to get them back now. Shall I do it? I said to her. Oh would you? she said.

'And I gave one long blow on my whistle and pointed at the playground and everyone trooped back inside in silence. How did you manage that? she said.

'Training, I told her.'

*

Almost exactly thirty-six years ago she lost a race and she doesn't care.

'Did you though? Did you really? Did you mind?'

You ask me this with such passion that I have to think for a moment. It's been so long since I've thought myself back into the loser's head, so long since I've felt truly unpopular. A pungent gym changing room. Knees veined and bruised. A bitten nail. A lonely desk, the wood ingrained with angry biro marks. No one in the seat next to me.

'Well maybe I did, just a little. To be honest, I can't really remember.'

'Look Mum, anyone would mind. Maybe you didn't like to admit it even to yourself?' *you remark with your fifteen-year-old mix of insight and brutality.*

'Maybe not. But you know, I wasn't very competitive in those days.'

You look sceptical and slightly uninterested.

'And you think you are now?'

I think about this and try to answer truthfully, but the truth is harder to see these days, especially when you're around to confuse me.

'I don't know. In some ways I suppose not, no. Are you?'

You shrug politely as if you belong to a separate, superior breed.

'Depends what about. Things I care about, yes, I like to be the best. I want to win if that's what you mean.'

'And what do you care about?'

You give me a weary grin.

'Nice try, Mummy. I'm not starting one of those conversations.'

'But it's important to be a good loser,' I say quickly and you laugh at me and pick at the spots on your forehead.

'Yeah yeah,' you say, 'but I'm more interested in winning.'

'I think that was quite kind though,' your younger brother says after a moment's thought, 'to wait for the friend. I mean, even though she didn't appreciate it One Bit.'

'I think it was mad,' says your sister. 'Mad but typical.'

'Typical of what?'

'Of what we've come to expect! Of the funny rules you have in your head, Mummy.'

You all laugh loudly and ask me if we can stop for a frappuccino on the way home.

*

When I was expecting you, in the summer and autumn of 1988, I swam obsessively, almost every day. I had to keep moving. It felt as if my life and yours depended on it. If I missed a day, I felt sick. Two days and I felt sicker. Somehow I had convinced myself that if I kept this promise to my body, then the dangerous, magical experiment that was having a baby would work out fine.

In a way, it did. I had you growing inside me and the only way I could keep myself whole was to keep on moving. I was the same with your sister and then your brother. Gone was the mousy child who was bad at games and in her place was a strong person, a Russian doll. I opened and shut easily and there was always another one inside me. Take it out and I made another. Open me up and there you'd be, satisfyingly round and small in the palm of my hand. That was the deal. Just in order to stay whole, I had to keep on moving.

You were born in January, your sister in January two years later, your brother fifteen months after that. None of you were accidents, all of you were planned, but you also sometimes felt more like a succession of brilliant ideas I'd had too quickly – one after the other, relentless and confusing.

Lucky you, everyone said, the perfect family.

I don't know how you do it, everyone said. Are you having any more?

It was summer. I was full of milk. My back always hurt. I had to exercise. I had to stay strong and I had to stay beautiful. The more babies I had, the more urgent this last one became. I would be perfect. I would make up for all the years before, the years in between. Furiously, I rubbed in oil, I stretched, I checked every part of me for marks, for signs of weakness.

*

The pool was quiet and expensive in a drab and reassuring way and full of old ladies. They swam in floral caps, white hair piled high inside, heads held erect, chins out of the water, careful, disdainful breaststroke. Businessmen dived in after lunch and made the whole pool rock, waves slapping the side. The ladies swam on, tight-lipped. I tipped over on my back and watched you move, lulled by the safe rhythm of the water. The attendants, unmoved by old age, business or pregnancy, read the paper, clean plimsolled feet on the counter.

A girl came up to me in the showers where I stood, a strange, tired double person, water streaming over me and you. She was dark-haired, young, pretty, thin-hipped, boyish.

'I just want to tell you,' she said shyly, 'you look great.'

I flushed and thanked her.

'I see you here all the time and you just, well, I'm full of admiration. You're such a great shape.'

She grabbed her towel and hurried into the pool.

I swerved away under the weight of the needles of water, horribly pleased. I breathed in the scent of shampoo, rinsed my pregnant hair, soaped my pregnant shape. You turned over inside me, playing amniotic loop-the-loop, and I cupped my hand where I thought perhaps your small head was and I laughed from the sheer excitement of it all, the big blue adventure of having babies.

I was winning. I was waiting for no one and this time I was deinitely ahead.

*

This is me, I'm six years old. It's a long time ago and I'm standing in a sack in the middle of a field and trying to understand what happens in this world. It's a long time ago but not so long that I can't remember. I remember everything. The field is green, it's hot, too hot and lines are marked on it in white — lines which you can see from far away but when you get up close they barely seem to be there. It's a puzzle for a person to work out, this map drawn on the world. Mr Jones did them yesterday, we saw him doing them when we came up here for practice. And somewhere far away there's the drone of a tractor, drowned out only by parents' cheers, the long note of a whistle, a teacher with a thing you talk into. It's called a megaphone, Mrs Rogers says.

It's very hot. I have freckles on my nose and a hurt knee where I fell down and quite a bad pain in my tummy. I get a pain when I don't like things. The pain goes when I talk to my Panda. Panda would like this field but not what we have to do in it. If I sat down right here I could pull up the grass and count the leaves looking for a clover that has four and let ladybirds run over the top of my little finger and think about later. That would be much more my sort of thing. Mine and Panda's.

I wish summer was over and we were somewhere else. Somewhere like Christmas.

*

Rerun the cine-film. There's Miss Hancock and Miss Betty on their antique upholstered chairs and there they sit in the flicker and the whirr in their dark glasses and holding their sticks in the dappled afternoon sunshine and look, up there, there's a big, spreading tree above them, branches gnarled and haphazard, blossom like candles.

'It's called a magnolia tree,' Mummy says gently as she wipes the corners of my mouth with her handkerchief.

'*Magnolia*,' she says again, pronouncing the word as if it were a very splendid and wondrous thing.

'That magnolia,' Mrs Hannah says, 'look at it, what a survivor.'

From long ago – a survivor and an angel, a candle, a dream. It will outlive each one of us, that tree will.

Soon it will be late summer and the old ladies will be dead, falling over one after the other, and there will be no more blooms, just the wasted wicks, the green leaves, the thick and twisting trunk, the perpetual cool its shade affords.

*

Here she is. Here's the child, the girl, the woman – so many years further on, so much more used up and grown up and, finally, running. Yes, running – she is running. After all these years, she's seen the point of doing it, of going faster than the rest, of teaching herself to get there. It's not easy. She's not especially sporty and, even though she always moves quickly, moves around a lot, she guesses she's not especially fit. Three babies. A life of sitting down and thinking, only her ten quick fingers moving across the keys. A slightly kinky back. She's slim enough and vain enough to be proud of her body, but her feet are as big as ever, her grip on competition as tentative and slight.

Just recently, though, she's changed. Life has knocked her right off track, undone all her certainties – the sudden cleanness of a blade hooked through wool. Undoing, unravelling. It's made her small, made her anxious. Now she feels as tight inside as six years old, as shivery, as unlikely.

She waits for low tide when the sand is hardest then puts on her oldest tracksuit bottoms, faded mauve T-shirt, Lycra running bra, socks and shoes. And she goes, now she goes. Moving across the shingle until her feet hit the sand, she's off, she's running.

The sea is smooth and calm, blue shadows moving over it as the sun tucks itself under the darkest, fattest clouds. There's an inky smudge over Walberswick — rain.

The dog runs along beside her, barking for pebbles to be thrown, but she ignores her. She ignores everything but the harshness of her breath in her throat, the slow bump of her blood moving around her body. She'll reach a point where she feels so much like stopping but she'll move on over it, she'll push herself past it and then — well, soon it will happen, the thing she hoped for, the reason she's doing this, the thing she came for.

A clean escape.

It will probably surprise her, coming when she didn't expect it, when she thought she'd really lost, suffered, given up and had enough.

But wait — because it's the one sure thing, this is. Just when she's least likely and least ready, then her thoughts will smooth out for the last time and her life will explode all around her and she'll be able to run on, forward, out of all of this, further than she ever thought possible — on, on, on into another place.

Acknowledgements

I could never have written this book were it not for the miraculously long memories of my former PE teachers Mrs Rogers and Mrs Hannah. I'm so very indebted to them both, not only for agreeing to talk to me after all these years, but also for somehow managing to remember this quiet, awkward mouse of a girl who was definitely Not A Games Person.

Thanks also to Mrs Higgins of the Nottingham Girls' High School for taking so much time and trouble to show me round old haunts. And last but not least to Nancy Hudson, School Secretary Extraordinaire, for rushing to the aid of an old girl with such generosity, warmth and energy.

One last thing. Lots of people have been telling me what a brilliant idea it was of mine to write this book. Well, it was a brilliant idea, but I'm afraid it wasn't mine. I owe it all to Tristan Jones of Yellow Jersey Press who had the perception (well, OK, it didn't take much) to realise that I must have been exceptionally bad at games – and the imagination to ask me to write about it. I never thought I'd write a sports book. (My family tell me I still haven't.) But the best editors make the most unlikely and magical things happen, so thank you, Tristan.

JSM, London 2005